Books by Volker Heide

No More Tears

God's Punch Line

The Key is Love

Let Go and Let God

Bless the Lord, O My Soul

Available on Amazon
In Paperback and Kindle

LET GO AND LET GOD

Volker Heide

King of Kings Publishing
Madison, Connecticut

4

For Wolfgang

6

Foreword

This is a collection of sermons that were preached in the parish. The good news of God declares you can have forgiveness and a new life in Jesus Christ. He is the Savior who deeply loves you.

These sermons look at many different Bible Readings and you are encouraged to read the passages listed beforehand.

God's Word is powerful and effective. The Holy Scriptures declare that God loves you. He cares about you and promises to provide for all of your needs.

Let these sermons lead you deeper into the Word of God. Read the Bible every day and study the Scriptures. There, you will find the answers you are looking for.

In God's Word, you will find Christ. He is the Son of God who comes to you with mercy and grace. Trust in him and receive his gift of life. Put your hope in him and receive his peace and blessing.

8

LET GO AND LET GOD

Featuring:

A STORY ABOUT TABITHA AND SIMON:
Luke 7:36-50, page 15.

YOUR GOD WILL COME:
Isaiah 35:4-7 & Mark 7:31-37, page 24.

PARTAKE OF THE BREAD OF LIFE:
John 6:25-40, page 30.

FOOLISH & WISE:
Matthew 25:1-13, page 35.

CHRIST = MESSIAH:
Isaiah 61:1-11, page 42.

ENGAGING OUR HEARTS IN WORSHIP:
Isaiah 29:13-24, page 50.

LET GO AND LET GOD:
Luke 4:31-44, page 60.

IN BETWEEN DAYS:
John 17:6-19, page 68.

WHAT KIND OF BRANCH ARE YOU?
John 15:1-8, page 76.

JUDGE JESUS:
Matthew 25:31-44, page 84.

LIVING IN THE VALLEY:
Mark 9:2-13, page 91.

THE TEMPTATION OF OUR LORD:
Matthew 4:1-11, page 98.

THE HOLY TOOTHBRUSH:
Mark 7:1-23, page 108.

WHERE ARE YOU?
Genesis 3:1-15, page 115.

FIRST SIGHT OF THE CROSS:
Mark 10:46-52, page 123.

HEAVENLY FOOD:
John 6:41-69, page 131.

THE NARROW ROAD:
Mark 8:27-38, page 138.

GETTING DOWN TO BUSINESS:
Luke 19:28-40, page 145.

A CHRISTMAS LETTER FROM MARY:
Luke 1:26-38, page 153.

Bonus Sermon:

A SHORT SERMON:
Mark 5:21-43, page 162.

The Spirit of the Sovereign Lord is on me, because he has anointed me to preach good news to the poor.

He has sent me to bind up the brokenhearted, to proclaim freedom for the captives and release from darkness for the prisoners, to proclaim the year of the Lord's favor.

He has sent me to comfort all who mourn, and provide for those who grieve in Zion - to bestow on them a crown of beauty instead of ashes, the oil of gladness instead of mourning, and a garment of praise instead of a spirit of despair.

They will be called oaks of righteousness, a planting of the Lord for the display of his splendor. They will rebuild the ancient ruins and restore the places long devastated; they will renew the ruined cities that have been devastated for generations.

I delight greatly in the Lord; my soul rejoices in my God. For he has clothed me with garments of salvation and arrayed me in a robe of righteousness.

Isaiah 61:1-11

12

Say to those with fearful hearts, "Be strong, do not fear; your God will come, he will come to save you." Then will the eyes of the blind be opened and the ears of the deaf unstopped. Then will the lame leap like a deer, and the mute tongue shout for joy.

Isaiah 35:4-6

Some people brought to Jesus a man who was deaf and could hardly talk, and they begged him to place his hand on the man.

After he took him aside, away from the crowd, Jesus put his fingers into the man's ears. Then he spit and touched the man's tongue. He looked up to heaven and with a deep groan said to him, "Ephphatha!" (which means, "Be opened!"). At this, the man's ears were opened, his tongue was loosened and he began to speak plainly.

The people were all overwhelmed with amazement. "He has done everything well," they said. "He even makes the deaf hear and the mute speak."

Mark 7:31-37

14

A STORY ABOUT TABITHA AND SIMON:
Luke 7:36-50

Today, I want you to use your imagination. I want to tell you a story about Tabitha and Simon.

Tabitha grew up thinking she was in charge of her life. She wanted money, love and acceptance. Tabitha didn't like the rules at home, so she moved out before she finished school. She didn't have much of an education and quickly found out that job opportunities were limited.

Tabitha soon found herself falling into a very bad way of life. She quickly lost her self-esteem and hit rock bottom. Her reputation spread around town and everyone looked down on her.

Tabitha wanted a way out of this mess, but she didn't know how to end it. In her own eyes, she was the worst of sinners. She didn't go to church. How could God even care about someone like her?

Simon, on the other hand, seemed to have everything going for him. He was a good boy growing up. He rarely got in trouble at school.

He knew he wasn't perfect, but he thought of himself as a pretty good person.

Simon got a good job and was a hard worker. He was well respected within his community and others looked up to him. He felt good about himself.

Simon heard about the teachings of Jesus and was interested. He even went to listen to Jesus preach. He wasn't quite sure if this really was the Messiah, but he wanted to find out more. Simon figured if he could talk to Jesus alone for a while, he would soon discover whether he was a real prophet or if he was a fake.

One day, after Jesus had finished teaching the crowd, Simon went over to him and asked, "Would you consider coming to my house for dinner tomorrow?" Jesus said, "Okay Simon, I'll be there."

Now Tabitha was standing there that day, too. She was standing nearby when Simon asked Jesus over for dinner. She had wanted to talk to Jesus, too, but she was so nervous and afraid. Tabitha had listened very carefully to the teaching of Christ and she was amazed. She was touched by his words and even stunned.

Jesus had talked about a father who had a son who ran away from home. The young man got into all kinds of serious trouble. When he hit rock bottom, he decided to return home to his father. To his great surprise, the father welcomed him back with open arms.

Jesus said that God is like the father in the story; God welcomes back sinners and forgives them. Christ then said that he was on a mission to seek out the lost and to save them. He said, "It is not the healthy who need a doctor, but the sick. I have come not to call the righteous, but sinners."

The next day, Simon set up for the dinner at his home. As was the custom, he would hold his banquet in a large open room. He would set the tables out and leave the gates open, so that others might see how generously he had provided for his guests.

Some passers-by might even stand in the courtyard, admiring the food laid out on the tables. The people might say, "Look at all that chicken and those fancy vegetables. Look at the nice loaves of bread!" (These statements would honor the host and not embarrass him. In fact, it was common that a number of people who had not been invited would stand around and watch the meal.)

While Simon was busy making sure everything was ready for his dinner, Tabitha was also busy over on the other side of town. For the first time in a long while, she had hope for her future. She now had a better sense of self-esteem. She felt a lot better about herself.

Tabitha had heard Jesus preach! She couldn't get his words out of her ears. She kept hearing the Lord's invitation, "Come to me, all you who are weary and burdened, and I will give you rest. Take my yoke upon you and learn from me, for I am gentle and humble in heart, and you will find rest for your souls. For my yoke is easy and my burden is light."

She was so overwhelmed by the power of his words that she gathered all of her money. She went to the store and brought the most expensive perfumed ointment she could find. She was determined to say "Thank You" to the Lord Jesus with all that she could, because she knew her life was never going to be the same again.

The time came and Jesus showed up along with other guests at the appointed hour. The people were admiring the food and the table setting. Then, as was the custom, they all reclined around the tables with their feet stretched away from the table.

Everybody was having such a nice time. However, as they were eating, a certain woman came through the gate. The people were all shocked. "Hey, look who's here. It's Tabitha!" Someone then said, "Just wait until

Simon sees her. There's going to be trouble for sure."

Tabitha ignored all of these comments. She goes straight over to the reclining Jesus. She kneels down and carefully sets down the jar of perfumed ointment. Tears stream down her face. The teardrops fall on Jesus' dusty feet. She takes her beautiful hair and uses it to wipe the dust and dirt off his feet.

She then takes the perfume and pours it slowly on the feet of Christ. She carefully concentrates, even though she is overcome with emotion. It's as if this is her final opportunity to make things right in her life. Jesus had given her hope and a chance for a new beginning.

As she knelt before him and cried her tears, she could feel his love and acceptance. She just knew that God had forgiven her sins. Now, she loved God so much because Jesus had come into her life.

The strong fragrance of the perfume filled the whole house. The dinner guests were all staring and looking at each other. This was very uncomfortable and awkward.

Simon didn't know if he should be angry at this woman or not. He knew exactly who she was, and what her reputation was. On the other hand, she might just expose Jesus as a false prophet.

In fact, as Simon watches her pouring the perfume on the Lord's feet, he thinks to himself, "If this man were a real prophet, he would know who is touching him and what kind of woman she is. He would know she is a terrible sinner!"

Jesus saw Simon's reaction to Tabitha and he said, "Simon, I have something to tell you." Simon says, "Okay, I'm listening."

Jesus said, "There were two men who owed a banker some money. One man owed him $5,000 and other owed him $50. Well, when it came time for the money to be repaid, neither of them were able to pay back the debt. Therefore, the banker totally canceled the debts of both. Now, which of the two men will love him more?"

Simon said, "That's easy, the one who had the bigger debt canceled." Jesus then looks at Simon and said, "That's a good answer. Now listen carefully. Do you see this woman? I was invited to come into your house. You didn't give me any water for my feet, but she made up for it, by wetting my feet with her tears and even wiping them with her hair."

"Another thing, you didn't give me the customary kiss given to a guest, but that's all right, because this woman kissed my feet. You didn't give me the honor of putting oil on my head, but she has poured very expensive perfume on my feet."

"Therefore, I tell you, it is because her many sins have been forgiven, that she has shown this great love to me. But whoever has been forgiven little, loves little in return."

There was a total silence in the entire house. There was not a whole lot Simon could say in response to that. He had not done any of those things for Jesus. Frankly, he was not ready to treat him as anyone special. A nice guy, to be sure. An interesting teacher, no doubt. However, Simon wanted to put Jesus to the test. He wanted to test him first, before he put his faith in him as the promised Messiah.

However, if Simon wanted proof that Jesus was the Messiah, the Lord gave it to him when he turned to Tabitha and said, "Your sins are forgiven!" Those words caused quite a stir at the dinner party. The other guests stood up and said, "Now, wait just a minute! Who is this guy? He thinks he can even forgive sins!"

The people all knew that God alone has the power and authority to forgive sins. However, Jesus let them know that he was more than a nice guy and an interesting teacher. He was the Son of God. He has the power and authority to forgive sins because he is the

Messiah who will suffer and die for the sins of the whole world. Jesus would die for the sins of Tabitha, Simon and everyone else.

Christ now looked at Tabitha and said, "Daughter, your sins are forgiven. Your faith has saved you; go in peace."

Tabitha had received the gift of God and that gift changed her life. She now had a fresh start. It wasn't the things she did for Jesus that saved her, but rather it was her faith in Christ that changed her life. She trusted his Word. She believed in him with her whole heart and soul. And she loved her Savior more than anything else in the world.

That is why she poured that expensive perfume on Jesus and washed his feet with her tears. That is why she showed her love for him in such an extravagant way. The Lord had rescued her from her old way of life and things now would never be the same. She had been forgiven much, and so she loved the Lord so very much.

But what about Simon? Perhaps he thought that there was nothing in his life that needed forgiving. Perhaps he thought, "Well, that Tabitha is a real sinner, but not me. I'm alright the way I am. I don't need to change anything. I'm fine just the way I am."

It seems that, in the end, Jesus didn't mean much to Simon. He certainly meant a lot to Tabitha, but not to Simon. But what about you? What does Jesus Christ mean to you? Is he truly your Savior, or is he just a nice guy and an interesting teacher? Do you truly believe his Word? Do you really believe it when he says, "Your sins are forgiven. Your faith has saved you; go in peace." Do you truly love him more than anything else in the world? Would you be willing to bow down before Christ and honor him with your sacrificial gift?

Today, we have heard the story of Tabitha and Simon. It is a story of a broken life and forgiveness, a story of missed opportunities and sad unbelief. It is a story of how the Lord Jesus reaches out to lost sinners. It is also a call to repentance and faith.

Let us take to heart what God says to us in his Word today. Let us ponder the story of Tabitha and Simon. Amen!

YOUR GOD WILL COME: Isaiah 35:4-7 & Mark 7:31-37

We begin with our reading from Isaiah. Listen again to what Isaiah says, "Say to those who have an anxious heart, 'Be strong; fear not! Behold your God will come; he will come and save you.' Then the eyes of the blind shall be opened and the ears of the deaf unstopped, then the lame will leap like a deer and the tongue of the mute shout for joy."

Isaiah speaks of a time when God would come to save us. God himself would come to undo all the devastating effects of sin. Our reading from Mark reveals how Isaiah's prophecy was fulfilled. Here, we see how the Son of God comes to heal a broken creation. He restores what has been damaged and ruined by sin.

Jesus restores hearing and speech to a man who was deaf and mute. He fixes what is broken and damaged. Our Lord brings healing and relief.

Think about it. Our bodies were originally created by God to be healthy. Our ears were created to hear, our eyes were created to see, our tongues were created to speak. God originally created us to be perfectly healthy and to live and not die. In the beginning, all of creation was very good. This world was perfect. It was free of sickness, pain, suffering and death.

Yet, something went wrong. Something terrible and horrifying happened. Something destroyed our perfect relationship with God. It brought brokenness into this perfect creation.

Why is there suffering and death? Because we have rebelled against God. We have turned away from the source of life and perfection. Sin brings brokenness and damage. It brings destruction and pain. It results in a loss of health and a loss of life.

The sad truth is that we have turned away from God and have broken off our relationship with our Maker. A wall of separation has been established, a wall between God and a fallen humanity.

This wall prevents us from seeing God's glory. It prevents us from hearing his Word and singing his praise. It shuts us off from his life-giving presence.

But God has a plan. He has a specific plan to deal with our rebellion. God will win back a fallen humanity and he will do it with grace, mercy and forgiveness.

Just look again at what our Lord Jesus Christ does in our reading. Try to picture the setting and situation. Jesus is traveling on the eastern side of the Sea of Galilee. Some people bring to him a man who was deaf and had a speech impediment. Jesus takes the deaf man aside and he leads him away from the crowds.

Notice how the Lord wants to make contact with this man; he wants to establish a personal relationship with him. Jesus carefully works to connect and to communicate with him. He touches his ears. He touches his tongue. The Lord enters into the silent world of this deaf man. He enters the quietness, the loneliness, the silence of separation.

Then, Jesus looks up to heaven; he sighs and groans; he shares this deaf man's isolation and pain. The Son of God now speaks his Word of command, "*Ephphatha!* Be opened!" And immediately the man's ears were opened, his tongue was released and he began to speak plainly.

Jesus speaks his Word and healing is bestowed. The people were astonished and said, "He has done all things well! He even makes the deaf to hear and the mute to speak."

The people were astonished because it was clear that in Christ, God himself has come to help us. Our God has come to save us, to heal us and to restore a broken creation.

The Lord of Life has entered our world of death, our world of pain and isolation. God himself has taken on our flesh and blood. He comes to save and restore what was lost so long ago. Imagine that! The Creator becomes a part of his creation. God has come in person to remove that wall of separation.

We see that so clearly in the miracle of the deaf man who was healed. Here is a restoration of health and wholeness. The silence is broken as Jesus enters into the world of this deaf and mute man. The wall of separation is taken down.

It is as if the Lord were saying to him, "I have come to take away your brokenness and pain. I have come to bear your burden and to carry your infirmities. I have come to suffer the passion and to go the cross."

That's what brings the wall of separation down. The suffering and death of the Son of God has infinite value and worth. Because here, God himself hangs on the cross. And the salvation he accomplishes is perfect and complete. It tears down the wall of separation. It restores health and wholeness and well-being. His death on the cross brings life.

Of course, right now, in this earthly life, we have this new reality by faith. By faith, we know we will experience the resurrection and the life of the world to come. By faith, we know that on the last day, we will be raised up and fully restored.

At the resurrection, our bodies will be raised from the dead and we will be completely healed; we will be transformed and changed. All weakness, sickness, disabilities and defects will be gone forever. We will finally be what God created us to be: perfectly healthy, perfectly righteous and holy, complete in mind, body and spirit.

Just try to picture that last day when all the dead are raised. Try to imagine living in a perfectly healthy body. Try to imagine the scene when all the saints are gathered together and all the people of God are reunited.

We will see our departed brothers and sisters in Christ again. We will be reunited with all the saints who have passed away from this earthly life. We will see our loved ones again. And we will see this deaf man who was healed by Jesus. We will hear his mute tongue speaking to us.

And the healed man will say, "It's all true! Christ is the Savior! He is the Son of God and the Lord of Life. He has done all things well. He speaks his Word and even makes the deaf to hear and the mute to speak."

Therefore, in the words of Isaiah, "Be strong and do not fear! Behold, your God has come for you and he comes to save."

You see, it does not matter what you are facing in your life right now. You might be dealing with isolation and loneliness. You might be struggling with hurt and pain. Today, the Lord bestows his wondrous love and grace upon you.

Christ bestows his healing power. He opens your eyes and unstops your ears. He loosens your tongue. Now, you can clearly see God's love revealed through the cross and resurrection of Christ. You can hear his Word of grace. You can speak the gospel and sing for joy. You can praise your Maker and Redeemer!

The wall of separation has come down in Christ. We are reconciled and restored to our heavenly Father. "God was reconciling the world to himself in Christ, not counting men's sins against them."

Therefore, rejoice and sing! Give praise to your Creator who loves you. Give glory to the Lord of Life who died and rose again for you. Give thanks that your God has come. And continue to live by faith. Lift up your eyes to see the day of glory that awaits us. "Be strong and do not fear! Behold, your God has come!" Amen!

PARTAKE OF THE BREAD OF LIFE: John 6:25-40

Nowadays we hear so much about diets and what foods are good for you and which are not. Experts give their opinions about what makes for a healthy diet.

Magazines feature articles on sure-fire methods to stay slim and fit. Infomercials tell us about special diets guaranteed to help us lose weight. It seems like everyone worries about the food we eat and how it will affect our body.

Here are few tips of my own. If something tastes good, it can't possibly be bad for you. If something is gluten-free, you can eat as much of it as you want. Late night snacks after midnight are actually fat-free. Chocolate cake, ice cream and donuts are a nutritious and balanced meal (at least for Lutherans). As Mark Twain once said, "The best diet is to eat whatever you like and let the food fight it out inside."

Today, we talk about food. We talk about the bread from heaven that God gives. Today, Jesus says, "I am the bread of life. Whoever comes to me will never be hungry and whoever believes in me shall never thirst."

Our Lord spoke these words after feeding a crowd of over 5,000 people with just a few loaves of bread and a couple of fish. Do you remember? A huge crowd had gathered around Christ to hear him teach. The disciples finally say, "It's getting late. You need to send them away because they are hungry." However, Jesus says to them, "You feed them."

The disciples respond, "That's impossible! All we have are a few loaves and two fish." Jesus says, "Give them to me." Then, Christ multiplies the bread and fish so that everyone could eat and be satisfied.

Notice how the disciples can only see the negative. They can only see how difficult and hopeless the situation is. They think it is impossible to help all these people. However, our Lord Jesus can do all things. All things are possible for God.

Think of all the people who cried out to Christ for help. Think of all the people afflicted with sickness, people struggling with pain and hurt, people burdened with guilt, people who felt desperate and trapped.

Jesus saw their need and he had compassion. He laid his hands on the sick and healed them. He helped those who were trapped in a hopeless situation. And he does the same for us.

Our situation may look hopeless and impossible. It may seem like things will never get better. We can only see the negative. But the Lord sees our situation and he cares. He understands what we are going through. He cares and has compassion. He reaches out to us in love, forgiveness and grace.

Think about all the times you were caught up in a hopeless situation. Perhaps you went to the doctor and had to take some tests, and all kinds of scary thoughts were running through your mind. Perhaps you are dealing with a breakdown in your family and nothing you do seems to help. Perhaps you are struggling with depression; you have so many troubles you feel overwhelmed and all alone. Maybe you are dealing with guilt and remorse. You regret many of the things you have done in your life.

We all have our story to tell. We all have those hopeless situations we have to deal with. But listen - whatever it might be in your life that troubles you, the Lord knows about it. He sees your need and he understands. And he is ready to help you get through it. Just as Christ came to the rescue of that hungry crowd, so he also comes to help us.

Jesus says, "I am the bread of life." Bread is so basic to our diet. Bread saved the people of Israel as they wandered about in the desert wilderness. Bread satisfied the hungry crowd as they gathered around Jesus. In the Lord's Prayer, we ask for "our daily bread."

Our Lord calls himself "bread" to show we can't do without him. Just as we cannot survive without food, so we cannot survive without Christ. We all need the Son of God to feed us. We all need his grace. We all need his saving death and resurrection. We all need to partake of Jesus, the bread from heaven.

And we partake of this bread not just once, but repeatedly. This reminds me of how we gather to celebrate Holy Communion over and over again. We feed upon the bread of life when we receive the body and blood of Christ. This is the food that endures to eternal life. Here is the true bread from heaven, the bread that gives life to the world.

Through this special eating and drinking, the Lord feeds our soul; he feeds us spiritually as we once again receive his grace. Through this eating and drinking, we are renewed and refreshed. We receive nourishment and are made stronger. The body and blood of Christ strengthens us unto life everlasting.

"This is the true bread from heaven, the bread that gives life to the world." Our Lord gives life to the whole world because he gave his life for us. He gave himself into death so that we might live. Through his sacrifice, we receive forgiveness. His body is given for us. His holy and precious blood is shed for the forgiveness of sins.

Without this sacrifice, we would be lost. Without this grace, we would have no hope. Without this love, we would have no life. However, with Jesus, there is salvation; there is hope and life. With Christ, all things are possible.

We now partake of the bread of life and discover that the Son of God feeds us with his very body and blood. The Lord is with you! He is there to help you in your time of need. You can cope with the troubles you face because Jesus sees your situation and he cares. You are not alone; it is not hopeless or impossible. Christ is with you and he will give you the strength you need to make it through another day. He will feed your soul and satisfy your hungry heart.

Today, Jesus says, "I am the bread of life. Whoever comes to me will never go hungry and whoever believes in me will never be thirsty. Come now and partake of my gift! Come and experience once again my love and grace. Come and partake of the bread of life and receive the food that endures to eternal life." Amen!

FOOLISH & WISE: Matthew 25:1-13

Back when I was in junior high, we had a star running back on the football team. He was a great athlete, but he had one problem. He would constantly fumble the football. Finally, the coaches had enough. They came up with a plan to try to cure the running back's fumbling problem.

They made him carry a football around for an entire week. He had to carry a football everywhere he went that week – at home and at school. That was quite a sight, seeing our star running back carrying a football all day long. Wherever he went, you would see that football. The plan seemed to work. He didn't fumble so much afterward. But you have to admit, that was very unusual.

Today's parable from Matthew also describes some unusual behavior. We see some girls who carry around not a football, but bottles of lamp oil. Our Lord tells a story of two groups of girls who run into unexpected events.

Jesus begins by saying, "The kingdom of heaven is like ten virgins who took their oil lamps and went to meet the bridegroom." And he ends by saying, "Therefore, watch - for you do not know either the day or the hour."

Here, Christ refers to his second coming, his unexpected return to this world. This is the last day, the final judgment, the end of the world. This is the day when our Lord returns to this world in full glory, honor and power. On that day, we will meet the bridegroom.

Today, Jesus describes ten girls on their way to a grand party. They are delighted at their happy prospects. All of them have been invited to the party. Everybody has their lamps. They are on their way to meet the bridegroom. The marriage feast is about to get underway.

Jesus then says, "Five of them were foolish and five were wise." The foolish girls took their lamps, but no extra oil. The wise girls, however, took some bottles of oils along, just in case.

Notice how our Lord turns everything upside down here. The foolish girls know that they have been invited to a daytime wedding. So, they analyze the situation and decide to take only their lamps with them. That is all they'll need, right? Nothing could be more sensible.

However, the other five girls insist on dragging along bottles of kerosene with them, just in case something goes wrong. That seems strange. Why would you want to lug around bottles of kerosene at a wedding party? That seems ridiculous.

Yet, Jesus declares the second group of girls to be wise. Why? What is going on here? What's the point Jesus is trying to make?

The point is this: If something can go wrong, it will. You can count on it. In this world, something always goes wrong. Isn't that true? I mean, just look at your own life. Think of all the unexpected events you have experienced. Think of all the twists and turns, all the difficulties, all the bitter disappointments and sad failures. Think of everything that has gone wrong for you.

And so, in this parable, Jesus now introduces just such a sudden twist. The bridegroom is late for his own party. The girls wait and wait. Where could he be? The girls wait through the day and into the evening. Finally, the evening turns into night and everybody falls asleep on the couch while they wait.

Suddenly, at midnight there is the cry, "Here's the bridegroom! Come out to meet him!" All of a sudden, here he is! The bridegroom has come unexpectedly.

Without a doubt, this is a parable about life as we really know it. The unexpected does happen and it happens on a regular basis. We are suddenly surprised by something going wrong for us.

That's when we react with all of our questions. We cry out, "Why is this happening? Why does everything always go wrong for me?" We ask, "Why, Lord? Why is there so much pain and suffering in this world? Why is my life so hard and difficult? Why?"

Certainly, these are big questions. But the only answer we receive is this: "Here's the bridegroom! Come and meet him!" That is God's final answer to us: "Here he is! Come out and meet him. Here is my Son, Jesus. Receive him and welcome him in faith."

This answer shows us how to deal with a world that always goes wrong. It is only as we wait in faith for the Bridegroom to return that all the wrongness of the world ceases to matter. Now we begin to understand that we can't solve all the problems we face in our life.

Furthermore, we cannot stop things from going wrong. We can't prevent the unexpected from happening. All we can do is live by faith in the Son of God who will soon return. We just need a simple faith in Christ as our Savior, no questions asked.

Christ is the Son of God. He is the one who dies on the cross for us. He then rises from the dead to give us a new and better life. What we need to do is just have faith and wait for him to return. We need to live in hope as we wait and watch for the coming of God's new creation on the last day.

Such a simple faith may seem foolish to the unbelieving world. To the unbelieving world, faith seems like bottles of kerosene you lug around all the time. People see us carrying our bottles of oil and they say, "Why on earth do you do that? That's so foolish!" They say, "Why do you go to church so much? Why do you take part in all that crazy religious stuff? What's the point? It all seems so stupid."

Faith may seem foolish to some. But faith, in the end, is the only real wisdom. Watch what happens now. The bridegroom is late for his own party. Everybody falls asleep. Then suddenly, the cry goes out, "Here's the bridegroom! Come out and meet him!" The time for waiting is over. He is now here.

The foolish girls wake up and trim their lamps. But they suddenly discover that all the wick trimming in the world is now useless. It is too late. Time has run out. Faith has now become the only way to distinguish between who is wise and who is foolish. The foolish girls realize this and they cry out to the wise ones, "Give us some of your oil! Our lamps are going out. Give us some of your faith!"

Sorry, too late for that. Time has run out, as it always does in real life. Our parable is telling us that there will finally come a point where it is too late to have faith.

Think of this way. Since faith is basically a relationship with God, there will finally come a point at which God will declare whether such a relationship exists or not. On the last day, God will tell us whether we have said "Yes" to him or "No." Nobody will get away with saying "Maybe" forever.

That is the whole point of our story for today. Someday it will be too late, too late even to believe. That closure is the final note on which our parable ends. The foolish girls are shut out. Those who are prepared and ready through faith, go into the marriage feast. Afterward, the foolish girls come and bang on the door. "Lord, Lord, open the door to us!" But he answers, "Truly I say to you, I do not know you."

Notice the Lord does not say, "I never loved you." He does not say, "I never called you," or "I never reached out to you." He only says, "I never knew you because you never bothered to know me. You never bothered to have a relationship with me. You never bothered to trust in me while you had the chance."

And so, all those silly girls lugging around those bottles of kerosene have now reached their final goal. The party for them is now underway. They have gone into the marriage feast. The wedding celebration kicks in and begins in full swing.

Never forget that heaven is like a fantastic party. It is the grand wedding party for all the saints. It is a great, unending celebration of joy, happiness and gladness.

It is the real life we have all been waiting for. And it is the end of everything that is wrong in this fallen world. It is the end of pain, suffering and death. It is the end of sadness and grief. No more tears! Here is the beginning of God's new creation, the new heavens and the new earth. Here is the resurrection and the life of the world to come.

Therefore, we don't want to miss out on this grand party. We want to keep on believing as we watch for the coming of the Bridegroom. We keep our lamps burning brightly as we wait for the coming of our Lord. We watch, hope and pray because it would be a shame to miss all the incredible joy and happiness that awaits us.

We keep the faith and we continue to lug around those bottles of kerosene. We put our faith in Jesus Christ, the Son of God, because we know our Bridegroom is coming soon. Amen! Come, Lord Jesus!

CHRIST = MESSIAH: Isaiah 61:1-11

Many people do not realize that the word "Christ" actually means "Messiah." They think Christ is the last name of Jesus, as in John Smith. Actually, Christ is a title like King or Lord. Christ is the Greek word for the Hebrew "Messiah." Both words mean "the anointed one."

In the Old Testament, prophets, priests and kings were anointed with olive oil. The oil would be poured upon their head. This would signify their installation into office. Being anointed in such a way meant that you were consecrated and set aside to do God's work. You were chosen by God to be his servant.

Over time, the title Messiah became a description of the God's great and final Chosen One. The Messiah would deliver and rescue God's people. He would be a great prophet, priest and king. He would be the ultimate Servant of the Lord.

It is interesting to note that our Lord Jesus was not anointed with olive oil but by the Holy Spirit. This happened when he was baptized by John at the Jordan River.

Peter says, "God anointed Jesus of Nazareth with the Holy Spirit and with power, and he went around doing good and healing all who were under the power of the devil, because God was with him." Notice how Peter describes the Messiah's work. God's Anointed One comes to rescue us from sin, death and the power of the devil.

Today, we look at Isaiah's description of the Messiah. This is a famous passage which Jesus himself read in the synagogue in Nazareth. He read this passage and then said, "Today, these words are fulfilled in your hearing."

Isaiah's prophecy is very carefully detailed. It describes the work of God's Messiah in terms of hope, forgiveness and comfort.

Firstly, Isaiah tells us that the Messiah declares, "The Spirit of the Sovereign Lord is upon me because he has anointed me to preach good news to the poor."

"The poor" – that describes us! Remember how in the Beatitudes Jesus says, "Blessed are the poor in spirit, for theirs is the kingdom of heaven." We are poor in spirit. We stand before God and confess our spiritual poverty. We are empty inside and impoverished. We need God's help. We say, "Lord, my life is such a mess! Everything is going wrong for me. I don't know what to do."

But here is hope for those who are poor in spirit. The Messiah preaches good news to the poor. He speaks a word of peace to our troubled hearts. He says, "Take heart, my child, I will help you. I will bestow my power upon you and fill your soul with peace and quietness. I will direct your steps and show you what to do."

Secondly, Isaiah predicts that the Messiah would heal those with broken hearts. He will liberate the captives and set the prisoners free. The Messiah will announce that God's favor and grace are now available for all people. "He has sent me to bind up the brokenhearted, to proclaim freedom for the captives and release from darkness for the prisoners."

When you look at the life of Christ, you see how he came to minister to the needy; he came to those who were hurting and broken inside; he came to seek and save the lost. The Lord comes to those who are trapped in their sins.

Again, that's us. We are lost and trapped. We struggle every day with our guilt. We are like prisoners who sit in darkness. But now the Lord comes to us "to proclaim freedom for the captives and release from darkness for the prisoners."

Sometimes we do feel like a prisoner to the past. Our guilt follows us around. The bad things we've done in our lives continue to haunt us. Guilt and remorse keep coming back. We feel trapped by the bad decisions and mistakes we have made. We are stuck in the past.

Today, the Messiah says to you, "I set you free and release you from your prison of guilt. I erase your past and wipe the slate clean. I now proclaim the year of the Lord's favor. Your sins are forgiven! Your guilt is gone forever. Let go of the past and live in the future."

Such forgiveness is possible because Jesus will go the cross for us. There, he pays the price for our sins. "God made him who had no sin, to be sin for us, so that in him we might become the righteousness of God." "The Son of Man did not come to be served, but to serve and to give his life as a ransom for many."

Isaiah also speaks of how the Messiah will comfort all who mourn. He is sent by the Father to bind up the brokenhearted. The Messiah comes "to provide for those who grieve in Zion, to bestow on them a crown of beauty instead of ashes, the oil of gladness instead of mourning, a garment of praise instead of a spirit of despair."

These are words we all need to hear. We have all experienced the death of those special to us. We all grieve the loss of our loved ones. This pain touches us deeply. The hurt we feel continues on for many years; really, it never goes away.

And it is not just death that brings sadness and grief. It can be the loss of a job. A divorce. The loss of our health. Moving to another place. It can be the loss of the world we grew up in and all the confusing changes that are happening so fast. We miss the way life used to be.

So many things can bring us sorrow and tears. We are all filled with grief. This loss continues to hurt deeply. Sometimes we feel like we are covered with ashes and a spirit of despair.

Listen. Today the Messiah says to you, "I will bind up your broken heart. I will help you to cope with your loss. I will fill the aching void in your heart with my presence. Remember, I have defeated death through my resurrection. I now bestow upon you a crown of eternal life instead of ashes, the oil of gladness instead of mourning, a garment of praise instead of a spirit of despair."

The Messiah speaks his word and his work begins. According to Isaiah, the Lord rebuilds the ancient ruins of our life. He fixes what is wrong. He restores the places long devastated. He renews our whole life and recreates us in his own image.

"For it is by grace you have been saved, through faith. We are God's workmanship, created in Christ Jesus to do good works, which God prepared in advance for us to do." "In Christ, you are being built together to become a dwelling in which God himself lives by his Spirit." "If anyone is in Christ, he is a new creation."

To use another picture from Isaiah, the Messiah takes us and plants us into the ground like a new tree. We become oaks of righteousness, a planting of the Lord for the display of his glory and splendor. The Father now chooses us to be his people.

God has a purpose and plan for each of us. He declares that we are now his anointed servants. We are called by God to go forth and serve other people. We minister to those who are hurting. We share the grace we have received. We reach out to others with God's compassion and grace. We all have a job to do.

Paul tells the Corinthians, "Now you are the body of Christ and each one of you is a part of it." Paul says, "We all form one body, the body of Christ. We were all baptized by one Spirit and have received the same grace."

That's amazing when you think about it. You have been anointed with the same Spirit that Jesus the Messiah received. When you were baptized, you received God's Holy Spirit. You were anointed with the Spirit and power. "The Spirit of the Sovereign Lord is upon me because the Lord has anointed me."

And now the Messiah sends you forth to do God's work. You are baptized and anointed, and the Father bestows upon you the power of his Holy Spirit. We are now being built up together to be God's new temple. God now dwells inside of you and empowers your entire spiritual life.

Because of the Lord Jesus, you can now say, "The Sovereign Lord has anointed me to bring good news to the poor. He has sent me to bind up the brokenhearted, to proclaim freedom for the captives, to declare the year of the Lord's favor, to comfort all who mourn and provide for those who grieve, to bestow a crown of beauty instead of ashes." Here, we follow our Messiah. We follow the Christ and humbly serve others in the same way he has served us.

The Holy Spirit will help you to do this. You can share the good news. The Spirit of the Lord will show you how to help others who are hurting inside. You can comfort the brokenhearted. You can speak a word of peace to troubled souls. You can share the hope you have in Christ.

You can say to others, "Let me tell you about Jesus the Messiah." You can say, "Listen, my life was a mess, but the Lord helped me. I was lost, but then I was found. I was trapped by my sins, but I discovered God's forgiveness. I once doubted God's love, but now I know the truth. I know that I am a child of God, baptized by the Holy Spirit, chosen and anointed by the Lord to be his servant to others."

This is the good news we all need to hear. Through God's grace in Christ, we can all say, "I delight greatly in the Lord; my soul rejoices in my God. He has clothed me with garments of salvation and arrayed me in a robe of righteousness." Amen!

ENGAGING OUR HEARTS IN WORSHIP:
Isaiah 29:13-24

One Sunday morning, a pastor noticed a little boy standing and staring up at the large memorial plaque that hung in the narthex of the church. The little boy had been staring at the plaque for quite some time, so the pastor walked up and stood beside him. He quietly said, "Good morning."

"Good morning, Pastor," replied the boy, not taking his eyes off the plaque. "Sir, what is this?" "Well son, these are all the people who have died in the service." Quietly, they stood together looking up at the plaque. Finally, the boy spoke again. "Which one, the 8:00 or the 10:30 service?"

For some reason, when we think of going to church, we think of it as some dreadful place that we have to go and put our time in. We hope that we will survive it, and not end up with our name on some memorial plaque.

Sometimes we come and just kind of drift through the service. When we leave, we have no idea what hymns were, what the Scripture readings were about or how many times we dozed off.

We all have Sundays like this, Sundays where our bodies are present, but our mind is somewhere else. We may physically present, but mentally, we are a million miles away.

We may even say all the right things, our mouths may speak all the rights words, our lips may sing all the hymns, but our hearts are disengaged from worship. Instead of drawing near to God, we are actually far away from him.

Such lip service is nothing new. In today's reading from Isaiah, we hear God say, "These people draw near with their mouth and honor me with their lips, while their hearts are far from me."

In Isaiah's day, the people of Israel would fill-up the temple in Jerusalem. They would come to God's house for worship. They would offer-up their sacrifices and sing the psalms. They would hear the Word of God, say their prayers and receive the blessing of the priests. They would speak all the right words, but still, something would be missing.

Their hearts would be a million miles away. The people were just going through the motions. They didn't really think about the words they were speaking. They didn't really feel close to God. Going to church was just something you were supposed to do.

And I am sure that if you had talked to the people of Israel who had worshipped like this, they would have said, "What are you talking about? I'm doing everything that God wants to me to do. I go to church every week. What more do you want from me?"

But then, God would say, "What I really want is you! I want for you to give me your whole heart. I want for you to draw near to me with a true faith. I want for you to experience the power of my presence."

This is a reminder that worship is about God and his presence. It's not about us. We don't come to church to be entertained or to visit with friends. Worship is about coming into God's presence. Here, in this place, we focus on God and not on ourselves. Here, we engage our hearts in worship.

Without a doubt, this takes a lot of effort. It takes concentration and work. But perhaps that is why we all have such a hard time of it. We often are just too lazy and indifferent.

Worship requires work. Worship requires effort and concentration. Here, we seek to give God our best. We give God our full attention, our full devotion, our entire self. That takes some hard work and sacrifice.

There is an old story about a small village in Spain. The people of this village heard the king planned to visit there. No king had ever done that before. So naturally, they became excited and wanted to offer a great celebration that would honor their king. But what could such a poor village offer?

Someone proposed that since so many of the villagers made their own wines, they could offer that to honor the king. Therefore, they each decided to take some of their best wines and to combine them all as one great gift for the king.

On the day before the king's arrival, they all came to the village square early in the morning with a large cup of their finest wine. They all carefully poured their offering into a small opening at the top of a large barrel. They were so excited because the king would soon enjoy the best wine he had ever tasted.

The next day when the king arrived, he was escorted to the town square where he was presented with a silver cup and invited to draw wine from the barrel. He filled his cup to drink. To his great surprise, he tasted only water.

What happened? It turns out that each villager thought to himself, "I'll withhold my best wine and give only water. There will be so many cups of excellent wine poured into the barrel, that mine will never be missed." And so, when all was said and done, the king was in the presence of people who simply went through the motions of showing their love and devotion to him.

That is what the people of Israel in Isaiah's day were guilty of. And we are no different. We also are guilty of simply going through the motions when it comes to worshipping our King. We don't give God our best effort. That is why he says, "These people draw near with their mouth and they honor me with their lips, but their hearts are far from me."

However, God also says in Isaiah that he will do something to change this. God promises that he will do something new, he will do wonderful things for his people, he will work wonder upon wonder. God will make the deaf to hear his word; he will open eyes that are blind. The Lord will give fresh joy to his people. They shall rejoice in the Holy One of Israel.

We know that all of these promises are fulfilled in Jesus Christ, the Messiah. He is the Holy One of Israel. He is the Son of God and he opens deaf ears and blind eyes.

Christ enables us to experience the power of God's presence. We can now hear the Word of God clearly. We can take to heart the wondrous gospel message of God's grace. We can now see, with the eyes of faith, the glory and majesty of the Triune God.

Christ changes our hearts through his gift of forgiveness, and that makes all the difference in the world. For example, consider how we begin our worship service. Think about what really happened in our confession and absolution.

We say, "If we confess our sins, God, who is faithful and just, will forgive our sins and cleanse us from all unrighteousness." And then, after we make our confession, we hear, "In the mercy of Almighty God, Jesus Christ was given to die for us, and for his sake, God forgives us all of our sins."

Think about that! For the sake of Christ, God had totally forgiven all of your sins –all of them – not just some or a few – but God completely forgives you. He totally cleanses you from all unrighteousness through the blood of Christ. You now stand before God as righteous, holy and without blemish.

This is what we receive from God through faith in Christ. "To those who believe in Jesus Christ, he gives the power to become the children of God and bestows on them the Holy Spirit. May the Lord, who has begun this good work in us, bring it to completion in the day of our Lord Jesus Christ."

In other words, God declares that you are forgiven and holy in his sight. God has begun his work of transformation in your heart. He is now working something completely new in us. God is doing something wonderful!

God is at work here in worship. He is working to make our faith stronger, to give us hope and courage, and to remind us what's really important in this life.

This is a work in progress; it is not yet complete. That is why we need to continue to draw near to God every chance we get. We need to allow God to continue this good work in us. Every week, we need to pray, praise and give thanks to God together.

In fact, after the confession and absolution, this is exactly what we do. After the absolution, we pray together the Kyrie. Have you ever stopped to think about what those words mean? "In peace, let us pray to the Lord."

"In the peace of knowing that our sins are forgiven, let us now pray for the peace of the whole world, for the well-being of the church of God and for the unity of all. Let us pray for this holy house and for all who offer here their worship and praise. Help, save, comfort and defend us, gracious Lord."

How you ever thought about those words, and what they really mean? They sum up everything we should be about. We pray for the peace of the whole world and for the unity of all. We ask for God to help, save, comfort and defend us. "In peace, let us pray to the Lord."

There is so much in our liturgy and hymns to think about. For example, the hymns we sing today are rich in Bible teaching.

Holy, Holy, Holy! Lord God Almighty!
Early in the morning, our song shall rise to thee.
Holy, Holy, Holy, merciful and mighty!
God in three persons, blessed Trinity!

Just as I am, without one plea,
But that thy blood was shed for me.
And that thou biddest me come to thee,
O Lamb of God, I come, I come.

Rock of Ages, cleft for me,
Let me hide myself in thee;
Let the water and the blood,
From thy riven side which flowed;
Be of sin the double cure.
Cleanse me from its guilt and power.

We praise you, O God, our Redeemer, Creator;
In grateful devotion our tribute we bring.
We lay it before you, we kneel and adore you;
We bless your holy name, glad praises we sing.

All of these hymns awaken our soul and lift us up to the heights of heaven. We join our voices together to praise our gracious heavenly Father and his Son, Jesus Christ. We rejoice that God has bestowed his Holy Spirit upon us and that we are his children.

The liturgy and the hymns help us to focus on God and his presence among us. The same is true for the Apostles Creed, the Lord's Prayer and all the other parts of the service. They all help us to draw near to God with a sincere heart. They teach us to honor God with our lips and mouth. We speak together what we believe. Our words reveal what our faith is all about.

But again, the danger is always present that we speak these words without really thinking about what they mean. All of us are prone to drift off at some point during the service. We all lose our focus. This is especially true with the Lord's Prayer and the Creed. They are so familiar to us we often say the words by rote. Our mouth is speaking the right words, but our mind is somewhere else.

I think that in this day and age of computers and technology, it's becoming increasingly harder to maintain focus. Everything is thrown at us so fast. We have some much information to process.

We bounce around between phone calls, text messages, e-mails, Facebook, Instagram, Twitter, YouTube, and everything else. Our attention span is shrinking. It's hard to keep our focus on just one thing. Our life seems fragmented into so many different pieces. This includes our attention span.

That is why the worship service is so different from anything else in the world today. This is the place where God comes to us in mercy and grace. God is faithful and just; he once again speaks his Word and bestows his gift. The Lord once again reminds us of the one thing we need the most of all – his gift of forgiveness, life and salvation.

Here, in this place, God says, "I love you and I care about you." God also says, "I want for you to give yourself to me. Give me your life and I will give you joy, confidence, peace, courage and hope."

God teaches us each week how we can engage our hearts in true worship. God works in our spiritual life to open our ears and eyes, so that we can behold the wondrous love revealed in the One who gave himself for us.

God says, "Behold, I will again do wonderful things for my people, with wonder upon wonder. In that day, the deaf will hear the words of my book, and the eyes of the blind shall see. My people will obtain fresh joy in the Lord and they shall rejoice in the Holy One of Israel." Amen!

LET GO AND LET GOD: Luke 4:31-44

Luke tells us, "Jesus went down to Capernaum, a city of Galilee. And he was teaching them on the Sabbath in their synagogue and they were astonished at his teaching, for his word possessed authority."

Jesus teaches God's Word and the people are amazed. His teaching had real power and authority. The people in Capernaum realize that there is something special and unique about this man.

In the synagogue that day was someone who also immediately recognized this power and authority. He cries out with a loud voice, "What have you to do with us, Jesus of Nazareth? Have you come to destroy us? I know who you are – the Holy One of God!"

This demon cries out in fear and terror. He knows he is standing before the very Son of God himself. Then, Jesus speaks his Word of power and authority. "Be still and come out of him!" Immediately, the demon has to obey. The man who was possessed is healed and set free.

Christ now leaves the synagogue and he goes to visit the home of Simon Peter. When they tell Jesus that the mother-in-law of Peter is sick with a high fever, he heals her. Then, Luke tells us, "When evening came, the people of Capernaum brought all their sick to Jesus and he laid his hands on every one of them and healed them. Moreover, demons came out of many, crying, 'You are the Son of God!' But Jesus rebuked them and would not allow them to speak, because they knew that he was the Son of God."

Again, notice how the demons recognize that this is the Messiah. This is the very Son of God! The people of Capernaum also recognize that Jesus has the power of God – he has the power to heal and save. They knew that Jesus could set people free and change their lives forever.

But what about us? Do we have such a faith? Do we believe that Jesus of Nazareth is the Son of God? Do we believe his Word is powerful and effective?

Do you truly believe in Christ as your Savior? Is he your Lord? Have you committed your whole life to him? Is Christ the most important person in your life?

In our reading from Luke, we see how Christ stands at the center of all the action. The Lord is teaching, healing, rebuking the demons and preaching the good news of the kingdom of God. It is just non-stop action.

In these 13 verses from Luke, Jesus is mentioned 28 times. He is at the center of all the action. He is the key to everything. He is the focus of everything that is happening. It's all about the Son of God.

What about us? Is Christ the center of our life? Do we joyfully confess that this is the Son of God, the Messiah, the Holy One of God? Is he the One we turn to when we need help?

In our reading, we see how Peter and his family turned to Jesus for help. You can almost hear Peter saying, "Lord, it's my mother-in-law. She is so sick. Can you help her? Please, Lord, do something!"

The people of Capernaum brought all their sick to Jesus because they knew he could do something about it. They recognized that this carpenter from Nazareth had the power to heal and save. And so, these people act in simple faith. They trust. They believe. They turn to Christ in a humble and sincere faith.

Most people today have a hard time living with such a faith. For some reason, we have a hard time believing the Word of God and trusting that God always knows what is best for us. We doubt God's Word. We are skeptical and suspicious about the Lord. We constantly question his wisdom and ways. Simply put, we do not trust Jesus Christ like we should. That is why we neglect him and push him aside.

Let's be honest. Christ is not the center of our life – we are. We think that we are the ones in control. We think we are the center of the action. We know all the answers. We know what is best. We don't need Christ or his help.

Instead of putting our faith in Christ, we put our faith in ourselves. Instead of relying on God, we rely on our own power. Instead of turning to the Lord, we turn to ourselves.

That's why we think we can fix everything in our life. We don't need God because we can do it all by ourselves.

But then, something happens that reminds us that we do need the Son of God after all. Something happens in our life (usually something bad), and we suddenly realize just how helpless we really are.

Listen. What we need to do is this. We need to let go of all of our foolish pride and let God take control of our life. Just let go and let God!

Just let go of everything that's wrong in your life and let God take over. Let go of your frustration, fear and worry. Let go of trying to fix all your problems by yourself. Let go of your fear and worry and insecurity.

Let God get to work. Let the Lord take over all of your life and you will discover something wonderful and amazing.

This reminds me of a poster that I once saw. It was a picture of a big handwritten memo. The memo said:

I am God.

I will be handling all of your problems today.

Please remember that I do not need your help.

If something happens in your life that you can't handle, do not attempt to resolve it by yourself.

Just give it to me.

I will handle the matter in my own way and in my own time.

And once the matter is placed in my hands, do not hang on to it.

Just let go of it.

Remember, I am the Lord, your God.

Let go and let God.

"Let go and let God." That is the message of our reading from Luke. When Christ arrives in Capernaum, he just takes over. He starts preaching and teaching; he's healing the sick and casting out demons, left and right. Non-stop action.

Then, the next day, Jesus says, "I must preach the good news of the kingdom of God to other towns as well; for I was sent for this purpose." That's how it is in God's kingdom.

The Lord Jesus Christ steps into your life and he says, "I'm going to take over now. I will be handling all of your problems today. From here on out, I'll lead the way; you just follow. You just let go and let me get to work. For I was sent for this very purpose."

I think we often forget what it really means to confess that Jesus Christ is our Savior. If Christ is our Savior, then it means we stop trying to save ourselves. If Christ is our Lord, it means that we stop trying to play God with our life. If Christ is the Son of God, then we turn everything over to him and we say, "I need your help, Lord!"

We say, "O Lord Jesus, I need for you to save me! I need for you to heal me and set me free from my sin-sickness. O Lord, cast out the demons that are trying to destroy my faith. Help me to trust in you again! Renew my faith, and help me to always put you at the center of my life!"

So many times, we want to handle our problems by ourselves, or even worse, we want to tell the Lord how to handle them. But what we need to do is just turn the matter over to Christ in faith. We need to call upon Jesus and let him act in grace.

This point of allowing Jesus to act in our lives can be illustrated in the following story. In a big textile factory, threads are woven into fabrics by complex machines. Above the machines, there is a sign that reads in big red letters, "If the threads become tangled, call the supervisor."

A new employee was working at his textile machine. The threads on his machine got jammed up and become badly tangled. Frantically he tried to untangle them by himself, but that only made matters worse. The supervisor came by and said, "Why didn't you call me?" The worker replied, "I was just trying to do my best." He then told him, "Doing your best includes calling the supervisor."

And so, in the very same way, doing our best means calling upon the Lord Jesus. We need to call him when the threads of our life get tangled. We turn to our Supervisor when we need help.

We trust that the Lord will act in our life with his power and authority. We know and believe he will work to help us. Just let go and let God!

Let the Lord preach the good news of the kingdom into your heart and soul. Let his grace take over your entire life. Let the powerful love of Christ renew your faith and devotion. This amazing power can set you free and change your life forever.

Today, Jesus Christ says to you, "I was sent for this very purpose. This is why I have come. Listen! I have some good news for you - you are loved! You are saved. You are healed."

"Always remember, you are special to me and I am with you! Go now in peace and live each day by faith and trust that I will help you. Because together, we have some work to do for the kingdom of God." Amen!

IN BETWEEN DAYS: John 17:11-19

An old story tells of our Lord's ascension into heaven. He is met by the angel Gabriel who asks him, "Now that your work is finished, what plans have you made to ensure that the good news of your saving work will be brought to the entire world?"

Jesus answered, "I have called some fishermen and tax-collectors to be my disciples." "Oh, I know about those guys. Not a very reliable bunch of fellows," said Gabriel. "What other plans have you made?"

Jesus replied, "I taught Peter, James and John about the kingdom of God; I taught Thomas about faith. And all of them were with me as I healed the sick and preached to the crowds."

Gabriel began to lose patience. "Lord, all this is well and good. But surely you must have other plans to make sure your work was not in vain." Jesus fixed Gabriel with a steady gaze and then said, "I have no other plans. I am depending on them!"

Our Lord is depending on us to spread his message of love, mercy and compassion to the entire world. As Jesus said, "Go and make disciples of all nations, baptizing them in the name of the Father and of the Son and of the Holy Spirit, teaching them all things I have commanded you, and lo, I am with you always, to the very end of the age."

Before Jesus ascended into heaven, he promised his disciples that he would send the Holy Spirit. He would give them the needed power to spread his message. The Holy Spirit would enable the disciples to be faithful and diligent in doing God's work.

This day in the church year is a day of waiting. This is a time for reflection. It is a time to stop and ponder, to listen quietly and pray, to wait and wonder.

In the sequence of things, last Thursday was Ascension Day, the day Jesus ascended into heaven. Next Sunday will be Pentecost, the day the Holy Spirit visits the disciples with power and tongues of fire.

Today is a day of waiting - a day to reflect upon all that Jesus has done for us. It is also a day to remember why we are here and what we should be doing with our time.

I imagine that after the ascension the disciples must have felt confused. They must have felt all alone and adrift, wondering what to do next. They had just seen their Lord go off into heaven. They watched their friend and teacher go away.

Now, they were all alone without their leader. They were in the "in between days." The Lord had left and the Holy Spirit had not yet come.

Our reading for today comes from a prayer that Jesus prayed with his disciples on the night he was betrayed, arrested and taken away. He prayed this prayer to comfort his disciples. As we look at this prayer of Jesus, we can also draw strength from it.

Our Lord says, "Holy Father, protect my disciples by the power of your name. I have protected them and kept them safe. I have given them your Word. Father, protect them from the evil one. Sanctify them by the truth; your Word is truth."

Notice that our Lord protects his disciples. He watches over his church and keeps us safe. The Lord is our Rock and Refuge, a Mighty Fortress in times of trouble. He is the head of the Church and we are his body. Jesus says, "I will establish my church upon the rock of faith. The gates of hell cannot prevail against it." Paul says, "Christ is the head of the body, the church."

Christ is also praying that the disciples would remain true to his teaching. "I have given them your Word," Jesus says. "O Father, your Word is truth. Keep them in your truth."

That is the key to making the most of our "in between days."

God's Word reminds us that we are safe in the Lord's ongoing providence and care. Our task now is to be faithful with what has been entrusted to us. Jesus says, "It will be good for that servant to be doing what his master commands."

It would have been easy for the disciples to forget all about what Jesus had taught them. They could have let the Word of God just slip away and disappear. It would have been easy for them to say, "Well, it's all over now. We are all alone. We are just a small group. What can we do? Let's just quit and go back to fishing."

However, our Lord wanted his disciples to keep the faith, to remain true to the Father and to believe in all the promises he had given them. Jesus knew the disciples would need lots of help. That is why he promised to send the Holy Spirit. With the Spirit's help and power, they could go forth into the entire world to share the good news of his saving work.

Think of it this way. Imagine a beautiful sailboat out in the middle of Long Island Sound. There it is - it bobs up and down as a brisk wind makes whitecaps. The sailboat is sleek and smooth, yet it drifts aimlessly in the water.

The power of the wind is evident, but the boat barely moves. Other boats zip by across the water, but this one makes no progress. It drifts aimlessly. All the wind power necessary was at hand. The boat was ready to go. However, it doesn't move because no one had the wisdom to raise the sails and set the rigging. Without raising the sails, there was no movement or direction. Without the sails, there is no way to harness the energy of the wind.

Often, we are exactly like that. Like the disciples, we have all the promises of Christ, we have the mission spelled out, we have the tools at hand, we have God's Word and the Sacraments, we have all of God's powerful resources - we have the sails - but we do not use them. We don't set sail and harness the power of the Holy Spirit.

The disciples needed the Pentecost experience and the guidance of the Holy Spirit. They needed the transformative power of the Spirit to get their boat sailing. They needed to raise the sails of God's Word and have faith that God was in control and God had a plan for their life.

We also need the same thing. We need for the Lord Jesus Christ to pray for us. We need the Holy Spirit to draw us together in unity so that we would not lose faith and drift apart.

We need to tap into God's power. We need grace.

That is the good news today. Jesus prays for us. He is with us as we face the "in between days" of our life. He bestows the Holy Spirit upon us and empowers us with his amazing grace.

"Holy Father, protect my disciples by the power of your name. Father, I have given them your Word. Protect them from the evil one. Sanctify them by the truth; your Word is truth."

Sometimes we feel just like the disciples did back then. We're not quite sure of the direction of our life. We do not know what the future holds and that scares us. We feel all alone and helpless; we drift aimlessly through life, with no purpose or meaning.

If you ever start to feel this way, remember these words of Jesus. Remember how the Son of God came to give you a powerful hope and a reason for living. Jesus came so that you might have life and have it to the full.

Even if you cannot get your boat sailing, remember that Christ is still your Lord. Your life still belongs to him. He died for you on the cross. He shed his blood for you. You were redeemed by the precious and innocent blood of Christ, a lamb without blemish or defect.

You might feel like you are lost and drifting aimlessly, but the Lord Jesus is still there for you. Some of you know exactly what I'm talking about. Some of us have lost loved ones, others are dealing with sickness and health problems, some are dealing with depression and loneliness and other issues. All these things can make us feel disconnected from our faith and adrift.

But the Lord Jesus says, "I have given you my Word. I will protect you from the evil one. I will be with you and give you the power of the Holy Spirit to see you through." Jesus says, "I will pray for you!"

Think about that! Right now, the Risen Lord is at the Father's right hand, praying for you. He is praying, "O Father, protect my child! Send forth your help. Have mercy. Surround my child with your solace and care. O Father, help my struggling disciple!"

That is totally amazing when you think about it. The Lord watches over all of his lambs and sheep. He watches over you and me and everyone else. He cares about all of his disciples. He wants none of us to be lost. The Savior is praying for you right now, praying that you would be faithful to his Word and strong in the power of the Holy Spirit.

As we live in these "in between days," Jesus is telling us to remain true to the faith and to do his work. When the disciples faced difficulties and hardship, they remembered these words of Christ where he prayed for them to remain in the truth of God's Word.

As we face the challenges of life in this fallen world, we know that our Lord is praying for us as well. We can raise up the sails of faith and tap into the power of the Holy Spirit. Christ will help us to be faithful in our calling. We can do God's work and share the good news of a Savior who loves us.

We can do God's work and carry out the mission, knowing the Holy Spirit will guide and empower us. Remember, the Lord Jesus Christ is depending on us. We all have a job to do.

So, let us get busy and proclaim the truth of God's Word! Let's get out there and share God's truth with the entire world.

Jesus says. "I am counting on you to go and make disciples of all nations, baptizing them in the name of the Father and of the Son and of the Holy Spirit. Teach them everything I have commanded you. And remember, I am with you, both now and forevermore!" Amen!

WHAT KIND OF BRANCH ARE YOU? John 15:1-8

Now that the weather is getting warmer, more and more people are planting flowers and working in their gardens. I don't know if you've ever had the chance to drive through those parts of our country that have large vineyard fields. It is quite impressive to see the huge fields of grapes and all the wineries.

All these vineyards would be very similar to the land of Israel back in Jesus' day. Back then, growing grapes was a very important industry. It was vital to Israel's economy. Everyone knew about growing grapes, and so Jesus used this to describe our relationship to God, our heavenly Father.

The picture Christ paints today is a simple one. Our Lord pictures himself as the main vine, and we are the branches that grow from him. God the Father is the gardener. "I am the true vine, and my Father is the gardener."

Then, Jesus talks about how God is like a gardener that prunes away the dead and lifeless branches. Jesus says, "He cuts off every branch in me that bears no fruit. If anyone does not remain in me, he is like a branch that is thrown away and withers; such branches are picked up, thrown into the fire and burned."

When a gardener is going through his vineyard, he may see lifeless branches that are not bearing fruit. Here is a picture of people who once were believers. However, something happened. They stop producing the fruits of faith. They fall away from Christ. They spiritually die inside. They become throwaway branches.

Why does this happen? How can this occur to people who once were active Christians? The answer according to our Lord: "If anyone does not remain in me, he is like a branch that is withered and thrown away."

Our Lord tells us it is possible to lose contact with him. It is possible to lose your faith and fall away from Christ. That is when you stop bearing fruit and become a throwaway branch.

Many years ago at the Tournament of Roses parade, the Chevron Oil Company had a beautiful, massive float. Right in the middle of the parade, the oil company's float came to a grinding halt and the rest of the parade with it. The problem? The float ran out of gas. The directors of the Chevron float had done everything well, but they neglected to use their companies vast resources of oil. The parade waited while someone ran to get a gallon of gas.

Too often, this is what happens to us. We break down in the middle of our life. We stop producing fruits of faith. Our spiritual life just grinds to a halt. Why? Because we neglect the one thing we need to keep our faith alive – Christ.

We lose our connection to Jesus Christ, the Son of God. We lose contact with God's Word and Sacraments. That's when our branch begins to die. We stop producing good works. We start living in all manner of unbelief and sin. Eventually, we will be picked up and thrown into the fire.

Our question today is this: "What kind of branch are you?" Are you producing the fruits of faith? Are you connected to Christ? Or, have you become disconnected from the vine? Are you a throwaway branch?

The forgiveness that Christ won for us through his suffering and death is the life-giving sap that makes us to be alive, green and vibrant. Forgiveness is the key. Staying connected to the vine means we are continuously forgiven in Christ. Now we are able to have a living faith which is active in love.

Ultimately, the Holy Spirit creates and sustains such a faith within us. The Word and Sacraments are the vast resources of power that the Spirit supplies to us. He fills up our gas tank every week so that we can keep on going. That is what worship is all about.

Jesus then says, "My Father cuts off every branch in me that bears no fruit, while every branch that does bear fruit he prunes, so that it will be even more fruitful."

One of the jobs of a gardener is to prune the branches on the grapevine. He cuts off the dead ones and trims back many of the living ones. Sometimes, the pruning is drastic. There doesn't seem to be much left of the branch.

All this cutting is painful. The pruning hurts. However, the reason the gardener does it is so that the branches can reach their full potential. Months later, they are able to produce a large crop of grapes. But this is possible only because the gardener did all that cutting and pruning.

God the Father prunes you. He cuts, he shapes, he removes those things that might harm your spiritual growth. He leads you to self-examination and repentance.

God the Father leads us to reflect on our spiritual life and our walk with the Lord. Is there something in my life that I need to change? Is there something that needs reformation? What do I need to confess to God and ask for forgiveness? How can I, with the Holy Spirit's help, amend my sinful life?

Such prunings are painful, but remember God prunes for your eternal good. He wants you to reach your full potential. He wants you to produce as many fruits of faith as possible.

Perhaps you are going through such a pruning process right now. It certainly can be difficult and confusing. Nevertheless, when it happens to you, trust that God is in control and the Gardener knows what he is doing. God is leading you through this process.

God's goal is that each of us becomes a fruitful branch. Jesus says, "This is to my Father's glory, that you bear much fruit, showing yourselves to be my disciples."

The fruitful Christian is one whose life is filled with good works. These good works include obedience to our heavenly Father. Even when the rest of the world is doing something different, we follow God's Word and his commandments.

Good works also include the way we treat other people. "You shall love your neighbor as yourself." "Do unto others what you would have them do unto you." Here, we seek to love and serve all people, including our family and friends, our co-workers, the people we meet during the day and even total strangers. "This is to my Father's glory, that you bear much fruit."

Jesus says, "Remain in me, and I will remain in you. No branch can bear fruit by itself; it must remain in the vine. Neither can you bear fruit, unless you remain in me."

No one can be a fruitful branch unless they remain connected to Jesus. It's all about Christ. "I am the vine, you are the branches. If anyone remains in me, they will bear much fruit. Apart from me, you can do nothing."

Without Christ, we can do nothing. But with Jesus, we can do all things. We can produce much fruit to the glory of God. But we need to stay connected to the true vine. Without him, we can do nothing.

The story is told of a native from a remote African mountain village who had the opportunity to visit a large modern city for the first time. He was astonished by everything he saw. He was especially amazed at the electric lights which he saw everywhere. Therefore, he got a big sack and filled it with light bulbs, sockets and switches to take home with him.

Arriving home, he hung the light bulbs everywhere - in front of his home, in his yard and in his neighbor's trees. Everyone watched him with curiosity and asked, "What are you doing?" He just smiled and said, "Just wait until dark - you'll see!"

When night came he turned on the switches, but nothing happened. You see, no one had told him about electricity. He did not know the light bulbs were useless unless connected to the source of their power.

Jesus tells us, "Apart from me, you can do nothing." We need Jesus. He is the Lord who freely provides the electricity we need to light up our lives with the fruits of faith. He has given us his Word and Sacraments. He has given us worship.

Here, we are once again connected to the cross and resurrection of our Lord. The Holy Spirit is at work to strengthen our faith. "Faith comes from hearing the message, and the message is heard through the Word of Christ."

So, what kind of branch are you? I have to confess, to be completely honest, that I am often a throwaway branch. I am a sinner; I'm not perfect by any stretch of the imagination. I stumble and fall all the time. And I know this is true for you as well.

However, by God's mercy and grace, we are redeemed and restored. We are reconnected to the true vine, grafted back onto the source of all true life. Christ has forgiven us. By God's grace, we are now able to begin to produce the fruits of faith in our daily life.

This is a work in progress, and the Father continues to prune us as needed. Repentance and confession remain essential. God's forgiveness in Christ is the key to hold on to. Remember, the Gardener's goal is that you grow stronger and closer to Christ.

Our Lord says, "I am the vine and you are the branches. If you remain in me, I will remain in you. Remember, no branch can bear fruit by itself; it must remain in the vine. Remain in me and you will become a green and vibrant branch, bearing rich fruits unto eternal life." Amen!

JUDGE JESUS: Matthew 25:31-46

Most of us are familiar with the TV show "Judge Judy." On Judge Judy, people take their grievances to court. They present their case and explain their situation. They give their evidence and lay out the facts.

Judge Judy presides over the whole proceeding. She is tough. She doesn't stand for any nonsense. She is decisive. Judge Judy doesn't tolerate any fools.

At the end of it all, the facts are examined and truth is separated out from falsehood. The final verdict is rendered. Some are happy with the outcome. Others are disappointed.

Today, we hear about Judge Jesus. We look at the last day and the final judgment. Today, Jesus says, "When the Son of Man comes in his glory, and all his angels with him, he will sit on his throne of glory. All the peoples of the world will be gathered before him, and he will separate the people one from another, as a shepherd separates the sheep from the goats."

And so, when all is said and done, we will be judged. When it all comes to an end, we will finally stand before our Judge. All the people of this world shall appear before Judge Jesus.

On that day, he will separate the sheep from the goats. The final verdict will be rendered. Judge Jesus will be decisive. He will separate truth from falsehood. He will judge all humanity.

Now, we don't like to think of Jesus as a Judge. In fact, the final judgment is something we tend to avoid. It makes us uncomfortable. We don't like to hear about unbelievers going away to eternal punishment. We don't like to hear Jesus say, "Depart from me you who are cursed, depart into the eternal fire prepared for the devil and his fallen angels."

We may not like it, but the Bible plainly teaches about the reality of heaven and hell. It speaks of the final separation that will take place on the last day. Believers will go to heaven, unbelievers will go to hell. One group is blessed; the other is cursed.

Another thing to notice is that the Bible teaches that the final judgment is based on our works. It is based on the evidence plainly in view. We are judged by the facts, just like in the courtroom of Judge Judy.

Think of it this way. On that final day, Judge Jesus will separate true faith from false faith. A true faith is active and busy. If faith is alive, it will produce good works of love and service to others. We will love and serve and give. We will worship the Lord. We will follow God's will for our life. We will obey his teaching and commandments. A true faith is always active in love. As Jesus says, "If anyone remains in me, they will bear rich fruit."

A false faith will be exposed for what it really is. Someone may claim to have faith, but the Judge will say, "Really? I never saw any evidence of faith in your life. You never worshipped me. You never prayed or read my Word. You never loved or served anyone. You didn't follow my will or obey my teaching. I see no evidence of faith ever being a part of your life."

And so, there will be a final separation on judgment day. True faith will be separated out from false faith. Believers will be separated from unbelievers. The sheep will be separated from the goats. Judge Jesus will render his verdict after looking at all the evidence. He will examine all the facts and declare the final verdict.

That can be a scary thought. This scares us because we know that our faith is not what it should be. Deep down inside we know that we have not been the people God wants us to be. We have not lived in love and service. We have not put our faith in action. We have not cared about others. Our faith has often been cold, weak and lifeless.

The truth is, even if Judge Judy was to look at all the evidence against us, she would bang her gavel and say, "I have to rule against you. The verdict is guilty." And, in the end, that's the correct verdict. The truth is this: we deserve to depart into the eternal fire. We deserve the punishment of hell. We should be separated from God for all eternity.

But at this point in the proceedings, something totally unexpected happens. Just when we think that all is lost, something amazing occurs. Judge Jesus actually comes down off the bench and he walks over and stands beside us. He then says, "I will take your place. I will pay the price for you. I will suffer the punishment you deserve. You are free to go."

You see, the One who judges us on the last day is also the One who dies on the cross for us. He is not only our Judge, but also our Brother. He is the Son of Man who suffers and dies for us.

This Judge became flesh and blood for us. He is the Son of Man who shares our humanity. This Judge takes our place. He is punished instead of us. He becomes guilty so that we might be set free. "For God made him who had no sin, to become sin for us, so that, in him we might become the righteousness of God."

On the cross, Jesus suffered the punishment of hell and damnation. Darkness covered the land for three hours as he was separated from the Father. "My God, my God, why have you forsaken me?"

Jesus was forsaken by the Father, he departed into the eternal fire prepared for the devils and his fallen angels. For three hours, Christ endured the pain and agony of hell. He suffered that punishment we deserve. He was cursed, damned and separated from the Father. "Christ redeemed us from the curse of the law, by becoming a curse for us."

Here's the bottom line. On judgment day, you will stand before the One who died for you on the cross. You will gaze into the eyes of the Judge who loved you so much, that he suffered all these things so that you would not perish, but have eternal life.

Then, the Judge's verdict on your life will be, "Not Guilty! Your sins are forgiven. You are acquitted. You are scot-free. Go now in peace and serve the Lord."

Forgiveness changes everything. Grace sets us free. We now realize the power of the cross. The blood of Christ washes away all of our sins. We are fully pardoned because the price has been paid. You are free to go. Case closed. "Go now in peace and serve the Lord."

Service is the final word for us today. Notice how when the Lord Jesus describes the life of a Christian, he speaks of works of love and service to others. Because we have been redeemed by the blood of Christ, we now seek to serve the Lord by serving other people.

If our faith is alive today, it will be active and busy. We will produce good works. The fruits of faith will be evident in our life. We will love and serve and give. We will worship the Lord. We will follow God's will for our life. A true faith is always active in love.

Such a true faith focuses totally on Jesus Christ. That is our sole motivation for service. In whatever we do for others, we say, "I'm doing this for my Lord. I am doing this to glorify my Savior. I am doing this in response to what Christ has done for me."

We see that in our reading. Those who enter the kingdom of God are people who were living out their faith in works of love and service to others. And the Judge acknowledges this. He says, "Whatever you did for others, you really did for me. Because you were a believer, you loved, served and gave of yourself for other people. Because you were a believer, you followed my way and my example."

And then, on that final day, Judge Jesus will say, "Come, you who are blessed by my Father;

come and inherit the kingdom prepared for you from the foundation of the world. Come and receive my blessing, the inheritance of the new creation given as a free gift. Well done, good and faithful servant! Come and enter the joy of your master." Amen!

LIVING IN THE VALLEY: Mark 9:2-9

"After six days, Jesus took with him Peter, James and John, and led them up a high mountain by themselves. And he was transfigured before them, and his clothes became radiant, intensely white, as no one on earth could bleach them."

Imagine what that must have been like! Imagine being alone with Jesus on that mountain. Imagine getting away for a little while from this world of trouble and turmoil, this world of pain and sorrow.

Sometimes we need a break from all the pressure and stress we face. We need some time alone with the Lord. We need to be with Christ on the mountaintop, away from the valley below.

You know what it's like to be in the valley, don't you? We all experience that feeling. We all struggle with that low feeling. We all have gone through the dark valley.

It may be a valley of depression and sadness. It may be a valley of loneliness and fear. It may be dealing with death and loss. It may be losing our job or facing money problems. We all go through those low points of life.

Today, our Lord would lead us up a high mountain so that we might be alone with him for a little while. That is what Jesus did for Peter, James and John.

He took them up the mountain, and there "he was transfigured before them, and his clothes became radiant, intensely white." Our Lord is transfigured before his three disciples. His glory shines forth in a brilliant light, it shines like the sun. The appearance of Christ is absolutely radiant.

In the Bible, the word "glory" basically means "God's presence." The glory of the Lord is his shining presence. In the Old Testament, this brilliant glory is often combined with a cloud. Thus, we see the cloud that covered Mount Sinai, or the cloud that guided the Israelites through the wilderness or the cloud that filled the tabernacle and the temple. This radiant cloud was God's presence veiled.

On the mount of transfiguration, we see a unique revelation of the divinity of Christ. This man, Jesus of Nazareth, reveals the glory he possesses as the eternal Son of God. He peels back his humanity, so to speak, to give us a glimpse of his divine nature. Jesus is true God, "God of God, Light of Light, very God of very God."

Christ is transfigured before Peter, James and John. His appearance becomes intensely radiant. Then, all of a sudden, the disciples see the glorified Christ speaking with Elijah and Moses, who have suddenly appeared. Now, the disciples are really overwhelmed.

Peter's initial response is to camp-out on the mountain and bask in the glory. "Rabbi, it is good that we are here. Let me make three tents, one for you and one for Moses and one for Elijah." "Let's stay here," Peter says. "This is great! Let's stay up here on the mountaintop and never go back down into the dark valley below."

What a turn of events! Only six days earlier, Jesus had been talking with his disciples about how he would soon be rejected. Mark says, "He then began to teach them that the Son of Man must suffer many things and be rejected by the elders, chief priests and teachers of the law. He must be killed and after three days rise again. He spoke plainly about this, and Peter took him aside and began to rebuke him."

Peter didn't like what he was hearing. He starts to protest, and says, "No, Lord! May this never happen to you." However, Jesus rebuked Peter. "Get behind me, Satan!" he said. "You do not have in mind the things of God, but the things of men."

Then Jesus called the crowd to himself and said, "If anyone would come after me, he must deny himself and take up his cross and follow me. For whoever wants to save his life will lose it, but whoever loses his life for me and for the gospel will save it. What good is it for a man to gain the whole world, yet forfeit his soul? Or what can a man give in exchange for his soul?"

Here, right before his transfiguration, Jesus teaches the way of the cross. Our Lord speaks of following him and losing our life. He speaks of taking up our cross and walking in his footsteps. When we follow Jesus, we are willing to accept the suffering and pain that may come into our life. We go with him through the dark valley.

In other words, you have to go through hell before you reach heaven. You have to go through suffering before you enter the final glory. You have to go through the dark valley before you can reach the mountaintop. The cross comes before the resurrection. Death comes before life. That's how it is. There are no shortcuts in the kingdom of God.

And like just Peter, we don't like hearing this message. We also want to protest and complain. The way of the cross seems so unfair. We say, "Why do I have to go through this valley? Why does my life have to be so hard? Why do I have to deal with this sadness and grief? Why do I have to deal with this pain and hurt?" We say, "Lord, it all seems so unfair! What kind of life is this anyway?"

This reminds me of an old cartoon I once saw. The cartoon shows a man sitting in front of a radio. The voice from the radio said, "This life is a test. It is only a test. If this were a real life, you would have been given instructions as to what to do, and where to go."

Sometimes we feel like that. We start to question God's ways and wisdom. We say, "Why me? Why this suffering? Why must I go through the valley?" But the Lord Jesus would answer us the same way he answered Peter: "If anyone would come after me, he must deny himself and take up his cross and follow me."

To follow Jesus means that we put our faith in him. We trust that he is the Good Shepherd and he leads us through this life. He goes through the valley before us.

We should never forget that our Lord goes before us. He goes ahead of us through the valley of pain and suffering. He shares our loneliness and grief. He goes through the dark valley, too.

That is the amazing thing about Jesus. Even though he is the eternal Son of God, even though he shines with the glory of God on the mountain of transfiguration, the Lord is willing to go down into the darkest valley for us. He willingly suffers all things as he descends down into the depths of our fallen state.

The Son of God is even willing to enter into the depths of hell as he suffers on the cross. Our Shepherd lays down his life for his sheep. He suffers that loss and separation from the Father. He is damned and forsaken. He cries out, "My God, my God, why have you forsaken me?"

However, on the other side of this dark valley, we see the light of Easter morning. We see the glory of the resurrection. After death, comes life. After suffering and the cross, comes something new and unexpected – the glory of the resurrection.

And the Risen Lord now declares, "I have suffered and died for you. Your sins are forgiven! I bestow upon you a new life. Now come and follow me! I will help you to bear your burden. I will lead you beside the still waters. I will restore your soul."

When we hear this message of grace, the true glory of Christ is revealed. God the Father confirms this glory when he says, "This is my beloved Son; listen to him!" That's what happened to Peter, James and John. They witness the glory of Christ and suddenly a thick cloud overshadows them.

Just like in the Old Testament, the cloud of the Father's presence descends upon the mountain of transfiguration. The voice then comes booming out of the cloud, "This is my beloved Son; listen to him!"

God says, "Listen to my Son! Listen to him as he says, 'I love you. I forgive you. You are mine.' Listen to him as he says, 'I am the Good Shepherd and I will be with you as you go through the darkest valley. My rod and staff will comfort you. My presence will sustain you.'"

And so, in the end, this is our true mountaintop experience. We hear the voice of God the Father and are reassured that the Son has done everything necessary so that one day we might enter that glory of everlasting life.

We know that Christ has opened the gates of heaven for us. We have this mountaintop experience by faith. The glory is yours today. You need to remember that the next time you go through the dark valley. It's only temporary. Fix your eyes on what is eternal.

"Therefore, we do not lose heart. Though outwardly we are wasting away, yet inwardly we are being renewed day by day. Our light and momentary troubles are achieving for us an eternal glory that far outweighs them all. We fix our eyes not on what is seen, but on what is unseen. For what is seen is temporary, but what is unseen is eternal." Amen!

THE TEMPTATION OF OUR LORD:
Matthew 4:1-11

One bright, beautiful Sunday morning, everyone in a small town in Ohio got up early and went to the local church. Before the services started, the people were sitting in their pews and talking about their week.

Suddenly, the devil himself appeared at the front of the congregation. Everyone started screaming and running for the exit, almost trampling each other in a frantic effort to get away from the devil.

Soon all the people were evacuated from the church, except for one woman who sat calmly in her pew, not moving. She seemed oblivious to the fact that God's ultimate enemy was in her presence.

This confused the devil, so he walked over to the woman and said, "Don't you know who I am?" She replied, "Yep, sure do." Satan asked, "Aren't you afraid of me?" "Nope, sure ain't." The devil was perturbed at this and asked, "Why aren't you afraid of me?" The woman calmly replied, "I've been married to your brother for over 30 years!"

Now, the devil is no joking matter. The Bible teaches that the devil is real and he is dangerous. The Bible says that the devil is a fallen angel, apparently one of God's highest archangels. He rebelled against God and tried to take over creation. About a third of the angels joined him, but they were all cast out of heaven. (These fallen angels are called "demons" or "unclean spirits.")

After Satan was cast out of heaven, he tempted Adam and Eve to join in his rebellion against God and we fell for that temptation. He told us that if we disobeyed God's commands, we could be just like God. We could replace God and be Lord of the universe. That, of course, was a total lie.

The good news is that God told Adam and Eve after the fall that he had a plan to restore a lost humanity. God would send a child who would be born of a woman. The child would grow up to crush the head of the devil. He would undo all the damage the devil has caused.

A few weeks ago, we heard about the baptism of our Lord. We heard that when Christ was baptized by John in the Jordan River, the Holy Spirit descended upon him in the form of a dove, and the Father spoke from heaven saying, "This is Son, whom I love; with him I am well pleased."

At his baptism, Jesus is anointed to be the Messiah who would save his people by suffering and dying in their place. However, if the Messiah was going to die for our sins, he had to be without sin himself. He had to be perfect (otherwise, he would need a Savior himself.)

And so now, at the very beginning of our Lord's ministry, we see how Jesus will face the strongest temptations the devil can throw at him. In the same way that a perfect Adam and Eve were tempted by the devil, so the perfect Son of Mary will be tested. Matthew says that after his baptism, "Jesus was led up by the Holy Spirit to be tempted by the devil."

Now, let me ask you a question: "Why did the Holy Spirit lead Jesus into the wilderness? Why did our Lord have to face the temptation of the devil?" This confuses a lot of people. What is the purpose of this 40-day testing?

Consider this story. Years ago, when the Union Pacific Railroad was being constructed, an elaborate trestle bridge was built across a large canyon in the West. Wanting to test the bridge, the builder loaded a train with enough extra weight to triple its normal payload. The train was then driven to the middle of the bridge, where it stayed an entire day.

A worker asked the builder, "What are you trying to do - break this bridge?" "No," the builder replied, "I'm trying to prove that the bridge won't ever break."

In the same way, the temptation of our Lord shows that here is the one man who can stand up to the devil and not break. This man fully obeys the Father's will. Here is the second Adam who succeeds where the first one failed.

Let's now take a look at each of these temptations. First, notice that Jesus fasted and prayed for 40 days and nights in the desert wilderness. He was alone and hungry.

The devil's main purpose here was to overthrow the Messiah right at the outset. He knew that if he could get Jesus to sin, that would ruin God's whole plan of salvation.

Satan waited until the conditions were just right. When you are desperately hungry, the opportunity is certainly present for sin. You may be tempted to satisfy your needs in ways that are wrong. You might be tempted to be dishonest, lie or steal.

The truth is there are certain times when we are more prone to temptation. The devil may tempt you at a time of bodily weakness, such as hunger or sickness or grief or depression.

Notice how Satan's basis for temptation was unique to Jesus. The devil says to him, "If you really are the Son of God, command these stones to become bread." Only recently at his baptism, the heavenly Father had publicly confirmed that Jesus was the Son of God. Now Satan uses that as a springboard.

He says, "You are the Son of God, right? Why are you so hungry? That's totally ridiculous. You should eat. Look, I'll be honest - your heavenly Father must not care about you, if he lets this happen to you. You should take matters into your own hands. Use your power to satisfy yourself. Eat something! Turn these stones into bread."

The devil was tempting Christ to act independently of the heavenly Father. He was seeking to destroy the Son's confidence in his Father's love. Satan was trying to get Jesus to doubt the love and care of God.

Furthermore, the devil thinks Christ should use his power to produce instant food. Of course, later on, Jesus would demonstrate that he could change water into wine, and multiply a few loaves and fishes and feed thousands. Christ had the power. Why not use it to help his situation? Here, we see how the bait is skillfully wound over the barbed hook. How will Jesus respond?

Christ answered the devil by quoting the Word of God. In fact, in all three temptations, Jesus appealed to the Word. That is the one weapon Satan fears more than anything else.

Paul says, "Put on the full armor of God, so that you may be able to take your stand against the schemes of the devil. For we wrestle not against flesh and blood, but against the rulers of darkness, against the spiritual forces of evil. Therefore, put on the full armor of God, so that when the day of evil comes, you may be able to stand your ground. Take up the sword of the Spirit, which is the Word of God."

We should memorize the Word of God and use the Scriptures to resist temptation. The devil hates the Bible and attacks it relentlessly. That's why you need to know and memorize the Word of God. As Jesus says, "Man shall not live by bread alone, but by every word that comes from the mouth of God."

Now, the devil tries his next temptation. He took Jesus to the top of the temple, and from that high point, he says, "So, you trust your heavenly Father, do you? Well, let's see how much he loves you. Let's put God to test. Jump from the temple and let God rescue you. Let's find out if he is willing to save you."

Satan was urging Jesus to be presumptuous and foolish. He was tempting Christ to prove the reality of God's love and care. This is a temptation we often experience. We are also tempted to demand a visible proof of God's presence and care.

For example, you might say, "God, if you don't heal me, I won't believe in you anymore." Or "God, if you don't get me out of this mess, I'm not going to follow you anymore." But that is not faith speaking. That is putting God to the test.

If you need to have a miracle in order to believe what God has already said, then you lack true faith. Faith does not put God to the test. Faith believes God's Word and that's that, end of story. As Jesus says, "Again, it is written, 'You shall not put the Lord your God to the test.'"

Round Two is now over. The devil is failing miserably. He now stakes everything on one final and desperate attempt to achieve his purpose.

Satan begins his third attack by showing Christ all the kingdoms of the world and all their glory. He then says, "All of this can be yours, if you will fall down and worship me. What do you say, Jesus, deal or no deal?"

Think about it, how appealing would it be to be the ultimate ruler of the world? The devil knew that Jesus was here to establish the kingdom of God and here is a shortcut to all the kingdoms of the entire world.

But Christ knew that the kingdom he came to establish was far different from any worldly empire. God's kingdom is spiritual. This kingdom would only come by suffering and dying on a cross. Our King will wear a crown of thorns. He would be mocked, ridiculed and taunted in much the same way that the devil tempted him.

When Jesus was crucified on Good Friday, the crowds gathered at the cross and they yelled out, "If you really are the Son of God, come down from the cross. Come down and we will believe in you. Use your power to save yourself!" They also said, "Look at him! He saved others, but he can't save himself. This is supposed to be the King of Israel! He trusts in God - let God rescue him now, if he still wants him. After all, he said, 'I am the Son of God.'"

Here we see how the Messiah is obedient to the Father all the way to the bitter end. He does not come down from the cross. He does not save himself. The Son does not use his power to turn stones into bread or to rescue himself. He does not test God's love. He does not rebel against the Father. Our Lord is totally obedient. He quietly suffers and dies for us. He endures all this for our salvation and for our victory.

Jesus' reply to the devil's third temptation was simple enough. "No, God forbids it." Jesus says, "Away from me, Satan! You shall worship the Lord your God and serve him only." Once again, we see how Christ puts his heavenly Father and obedience to his will above everything else.

The final round of this conflict in the desert is over. Jesus was victorious over the most powerful temptations the devil could throw at him. Because Jesus resisted all of these temptations, he could issue the command, "Be gone, Satan!"

Matthew says, "Then, the devil left him and angels came and ministered to him." (These are the good angels who do God's work.)

The good news today is that we share in our Lord's victory over the devil. James says, "Resist the devil, and he will flee from you." Paul says, "No temptation has seized you except what is common to everyone. And God is faithful; he will not let you be tempted beyond what you bear. But when you are tempted, he will also provide a way out, so that you can stand up under it."

Christ has won the victory here in the wilderness. He was now ready to begin his ministry. He will now call others to follow him. He will preach and teach and heal the sick. He will establish God's kingdom through his love and service. Our King will offer up himself as the final sacrifice for sin.

The key for us is to keep on believing in Christ as our King and Savior. Then, we can receive his victory and stand firm in the faith. We can put on the full armor of God and take up the sword of the Spirit, which is the Word of God.

Now, you can live each day knowing that you are safe in God's love. He cares for you and he will help you to live in obedience to his will. He will teach you how to live by faith each day.

Peter says, "Humble yourselves under God's mighty hand so that he may lift you up in due time. Cast all your anxiety on him because he cares for you. Be self-controlled and alert. Your enemy the devil prowls around like a roaring lion. Resist him, standing firm in your faith." Amen!

THE HOLY TOOTHBRUSH: Mark 7:1-23

We use many words in church that people may not fully understand. Often, they are big words like redemption, justification, sanctification, eschatology, atonement or propitiation. And when we want to really sound theological, we can combine a few of them, like forensic justification or substitutionary atonement.

Each one of these words is important. They have great meaning for us because they describe important aspects of our Christian faith. The problem is when we use such technical jargon in our preaching and teaching, the meaning often gets lost.

There is a simple four-letter word that falls into this category. It is a common word in the Bible, but one that is hard to pin down. It is at the core of today's reading. That word is "holy."

In the Bible, the word "holy" basically means something that is set apart for God, something dedicated to a special usage, something consecrated for service to the Lord.

Please note that being "holy" is a condition bestowed by God. It is not something we create or attain. It is something God initiates.

In today's reading, the lack of holiness is easy to describe. The word that describes the opposite of "holy" is "defiled."

There is an easy illustration of what being holy and defiled means. It uses a common item in your house, a toothbrush. Picture in your mind, a brand new toothbrush, still in its original store package.

When you open the package, you have a brand-new, unused toothbrush, all ready to go. At this point, it is a holy toothbrush. It is "clean" and "holy." It is specifically set aside to be used for one specific job – to brush your teeth and your teeth only.

Now, if you were to take your holy toothbrush and use it to brush your dog's teeth, then, that toothbrush would be "defiled." It would now be "unclean" and unfit for you to use. (You could probably still use it, but it would defile your mouth with dog germs. It would make your mouth "unclean" and "unholy.")

The defiled dog toothbrush could possibly be made clean once again by washing it with soap and boiling water. It could be restored to its original purpose if some kind of thorough cleansing process takes place.

Hopefully, by now, you can see where this is going. Today, we see how our Lord Jesus describes our problem of "being unclean" and "unholy." He tells us that our sinfulness makes us unclean. We are no longer in the original spiritual state in which God created us. We are sinners. We are unholy and defiled. We are dog toothbrushes.

Today, our Lord encounters a group of Pharisees who insist that being unclean is an outward condition that can be easily fixed by doing some outward activities, such as washing your hands or fasting or doing some other self-devised action.

Somewhere along the way, the Pharisees started to assume that spiritual holiness depended on us fixing the problem. They thought we have the ability to do something to make ourselves clean and holy.

However, as Jesus will point out, the problem runs much deeper than we realize. It's not so easy for us to fix this. The problem is deep down inside of us. Our sinful heart is the core problem here; it is the root and cause of sinful actions. What's inside of us is reflected on the outside. In other words, we do sinful actions because we are sinners by nature.

Furthermore, a dog toothbrush cannot change itself back into a human toothbrush. It will stay a dog toothbrush until somebody picks it up, takes it to the kitchen sink and thoroughly cleans it. The point here is that we need for someone to step into the picture and fix this problem for us. We need grace. The toothbrush by itself can do nothing.

Listen now to what our Lord Jesus says. Mark tells us, "Again Jesus called the crowd to him and said, 'Listen to me. Nothing outside a man can make him unclean by going into him. Rather, it is what comes out of a man that makes him unclean.'"

Jesus then went on and said, "What comes out of a person is what makes them unclean. For from within, out of people's hearts, come evil thoughts, sexual immorality, theft, murder, adultery, greed, malice, deceit, lewdness, envy, slander, arrogance and folly. All these evils come from inside and make a person unclean."

You see, our problem of being unholy is a spiritual problem. "All these evils come from inside and make us unclean." All these sinful attitudes and actions show that we have a spiritual problem that needs to be dealt with. We need to become clean, to become holy, to be restored to the original purpose we were created for.

The Pharisees thought we could make ourselves holy. They thought that outward actions could remedy our malady. But that's not the way to real sanctification and holiness.

The only way to real holiness is through Jesus Christ, the Holy One of God. He is the one who makes us clean and holy, from the inside out. We need to be born again, recreated and totally renewed. Here's how that happens.

Our Lord takes our uncleanness upon himself. He takes up and carries all of our sin and guilt. He heaps all of our evil upon himself and he takes it all to the cross. Christ will die on the cross so that we might receive cleansing and forgiveness.

Paul says, "Christ redeemed us from the curse of the law, by becoming a curse for us." "God made him who had no sin, to be sin for us, so that in him, we might become the righteousness of God." In other words, "God made the Holy One who had no sin to become the Unholy One. He carried our sins for us and became unholy so that we might receive the holiness of God as a free gift."

Simply put, Jesus died on the cross to pay the price for all of our evil thoughts, for our sexual immorality, theft, murder, adultery, greed, malice, deceit, lewdness, envy, slander, arrogance, folly and everything else that is wrong in our life. The Son of God takes our place, dies our death and suffers the punishment we deserve.

This is called our Lord's "substitutionary atonement," and it enables us to be "forensically justified." In less technical terms, our Savior has taken all of our filth and evil upon himself so that we might be declared clean and holy by God.

Christ took our place and paid the price for our salvation. God now declares that our sins are forgiven. By God's grace, we are restored back to our original purpose. God does for us something we could never achieve on our own.

Listen to Paul's description of this in Ephesians: "Christ loved the church and gave himself up for her to make her holy, cleansing her by the washing with water through the word, and to present her to himself as a radiant church, without stain or wrinkle or any other blemish, but holy and blameless."

Here is a clear reference to the cross of Jesus and our baptism. In baptism, we were forgiven and declared holy. We were "cleansed by the washing with water through the word." We were washed clean with the blood of Jesus and purified. "The blood of Jesus, God's Son, purifies us from all sin." "He is faithful and just and will forgive us our sins and purify us from all unrighteousness."

This is something to celebrate, something to rejoice in! For that which was defiled has been made pure and holy. You have been redeemed and restored. "This is not of yourselves, it is the gift of God. Not by works, so that no can boast." The dog toothbrush is now a human toothbrush again!

By God's grace and mercy, we are now declared holy and clean. We are again set apart for a specific purpose – not to clean teeth, but to be people of God. This means we seek to love God and to love others. We love other people in the same way that Christ loved us. We are now set apart for service, consecrated to be the people of God.

Listen, you have been born again by the grace of God. You have been washed, cleansed, redeemed and made holy. "God saved us through the washing of rebirth and renewal by the Holy Spirit." "The Spirit of Glory now rests on you." "You were washed, you were sanctified, you were justified in the name of the Lord Jesus Christ and by the Spirit of our God."

This is something to celebrate and be thankful for. The Holy Spirit is the one who makes us holy. He helps us to lead a godly life. He directs and empowers us to follow the way of Christ. He makes us to be a holy toothbrush, fresh out of the package, all ready to go. Amen!

WHERE ARE YOU? Genesis 3:1-15.

In a recent telephone survey, parents were asked the question, "If you had to do it all over again, would you have children?" A number of people answered, "No, definitely not. I would not have any children." That is surprising!

Here's what I think happened. I bet the telephone survey called the house at around dinnertime, after a long and frustrating day. I can just picture a tired and worn-out parent answering the phone. The kids are yelling and screaming and running all around the house.

"What's that you say? How would I feel if my kids ran away from home? I don't know. Happy? Elated? Relieved?"

Being a parent is a tough job. It's not so easy dealing with our kids. Our children misbehave. They disobey; they never listen to what we say.

That is the situation in our reading from Genesis. God had created Adam and Eve in his own image. He had given them a perfect home to live in. He had provided for their every need. God had done everything possible so that they might be happy, safe and secure. And how did Adam and Eve repay God?

The children disobeyed. They rebelled. They refused to listen to what God had told them. Adam and Eve were ungrateful for all that God had done for them. They didn't realize how good they had it. They thought they could do better. They insisted on going their own way.

And so now, we see what happens after the fall of Adam and Eve. We see how the Lord God is walking in the Garden of Eden in the cool of the day. Watch what happens now.

Adam and Eve know that God is coming their way. So what do they do? They run and hide among the bushes and trees. They try to disappear into the dense undergrowth. You can just picture them crouching down in the thick bushes, whispering to themselves, "God will never find us here!"

So, what does God do? How does God respond? The Lord God called to them, saying, "Where are you?"

Why does God call out like this and search for Adam and Eve? Doesn't he know where they are? Can't God see them hiding in the bushes? God acts as if he doesn't know what's going on. Here, we see God coming down to our level. Like a parent trying to communicate with a rebellious young child, God lowers himself down to our level.

Like a parent reaching out a disobedient child, God calls Adam and Eve out of the bushes. He calls them forth because he wants them to confess their sin and come clean. God wants for them to admit they did something wrong.

Like a caring parent, God desires what is best for his children. That is why he calls out to us, too. God calls for us to confess our sin so that we might come clean and admit our wrongdoing.

But that's so hard for us to do, isn't it? We run and hide and pretend we did nothing wrong. Just look at how Adam and Eve react after the fall.

First, they try to hide from God. They try to cover up their shame and nakedness with fig leaves. They run away from God's presence and think they can hide and escape God's notice.

Even after God calls them forth, Adam and Eve pass the buck. They blame someone else. It's not their fault. The Lord God says, "Why are you hiding in the bushes?" Adam says, "I heard the sound of you walking in the garden, and I was afraid because I'm naked; so, I hid myself."

God then says, "Who told you that you were naked? Have you eaten of the tree of which I commanded you not to eat?" Adam then points to Eve, and says, "This woman whom you gave to be with me, she gave me fruit of the tree, and I ate."

Adam basically says, "Look, God, this whole woman thing was your idea. This is all your fault! The woman whom you gave me, she told me to do it."

Notice how Adam blames not only Eve, but also God. But like a patient parent, God does not respond to this childish accusation. Instead, God turns to Eve. "Okay, what is this you have done?" Eve points to the snake, and says, "The serpent deceived me and I ate." Eve says, "It's not my fault! The devil made me do it."

Now, there is a grain of truth in that. The devil does deceive us into thinking that we can disobey God and no harm will come of it. The devil convinces us that we can run our life better than God can. We think we can do whatever we want. We can rebel and disobey and misbehave, just like a bunch of spoiled teenagers.

Here's the bottom line to all of this. It amazes me that God is so patient with us. Time and time again, God calls out to us through his Word and the Holy Spirit. We get ourselves in trouble, we mess up our life, we fall into all manner of sin, and still, God calls out, "Where are you?"

The Lord God calls to us; he searches and finds us and brings us out of the bushes, and he says, "What is this you have done?" You see, God is reaching out to us in love. He desires what is best for us. God wants for us to be honest with him, to come clean and admit our guilt. We have done what is wrong. We have disobeyed. Deep down inside, we know that's true.

God calls out to us and he leads us to repentance. Then, for the sake of Christ, God bestows his grace. For the sake of the offspring of the woman, God forgives all of our sins. Because of Mary's Son, God declares that the devil is defeated and crushed. If you listen carefully to what God says at the end of our text, you will hear the first gospel promise in the Bible.

The Lord God said to the serpent, "I will put enmity between you and the woman, and between your offspring and her offspring; he shall crush your head, and you shall bruise his heel."

Already in the Garden of Eden, God gives Adam and Eve the promise that one day an offspring of the woman will crush the head of the serpent. One day, someone born of the woman will totally crush the devil and defeat him and undo all the damage he caused in the Garden of Eden. However, in the process, the serpent will strike the heel of the woman's son. This is a reference to the passion of our Lord.

The devil would inflict a deadly blow upon the Son of Mary. It will seem as if all is lost when our Lord is betrayed into the hands of sinners, when he is condemned and crucified. The Son of Mary suffers terribly and dies on the cross. The serpent strikes him with a vicious blow.

But God's victory comes only through the suffering and death of his Son. The one born of the virgin Mary must take upon himself our sin and guilt and wrongdoing. He must pay the price for our rebellion.

Jesus Christ is the promised offspring of Eve. He is the Messiah that all of the people of the Old Testament were looking for. Even Adam and Eve would put their faith in the coming Savior. They were looking forward to the coming Messiah who would restore a broken creation. They longed for the Savior who would undo all the damage the fall had caused.

Again, this promised one is Jesus of Nazareth. He takes our place upon the cross and suffers the punishment we deserve. That is why, for the sake of Christ, God bestows his grace upon us. That is why the Lord God seeks out and searches for those who are lost. He calls out, "Where are you?"

This is the special work of the Holy Spirit who calls, gathers and enlightens lost sinners like you and me. The Holy Spirit calls us through the gospel. He brings us to the cross and empty tomb. There, he richly and daily forgives all of our sins. And the Holy Spirit is also working to change us from spoiled teenagers into mature adults. The Spirit helps us grow in our faith.

In the same way that God reached out to Adam and Eve after the fall, God continues to reach out to us today. The Lord God calls out, *"Wo bist du?"* That is how the German Bible reads it: *"Wo bist du?"* ("Where are you?")

Just like a parent calling a child who is playing outside in the backyard, God calls out in a loud voice, *"Wo bist du?"* Those words bring back many memories for me. My mother would use those exact words to call me. *"Volker, wo bist du?"*

I'm sure that all of us have memories of being a child and playing in the backyard or neighborhood. Then, we hear the voice of our mother or father calling for us to come inside. "Where are you? Time to come home! Dinner is ready!"

The good news today is that the heavenly Father is calling out to you. The Father reaches out in grace and he says, "Listen, you are my child! You are mine forevermore. Come now and receive my gift of grace. Come on home and join me for dinner. And always remember that I love you and I want you to be with me, both now and forever." Amen!

FIRST SIGHT OF THE CROSS: Mark 10:46-52

It is hard for us to imagine the anticipation of the crowds that followed Jesus as he went up to Jerusalem for the last time. The buildup of their expectation was something you could almost feel. There was electricity in the air. Everyone knew that something special was about to happen.

Great crowds of people were streaming towards Jerusalem for the yearly celebration of the Passover. Jesus was also going there to celebrate the festival with his disciples. However, he was also going there for another specific reason.

Earlier, Jesus told his disciples, "We are going up to Jerusalem and the Son of Man will be betrayed to the chief priests and teachers of the law. They will condemn him to death and will hand him over to the Gentiles who will mock him and spit on him, flog him and kill him. Three days later he will rise."

Jesus plainly told his disciples why he was going to Jerusalem for the last time, but the disciples really did not understand what he was saying. They couldn't see what Christ was talking about. They were spiritually blind when it came to the teaching of the cross.

As the Lord begins his final approach to Jerusalem, he comes to the great city of Jericho. This was an ancient city with a long history. It was about 20 miles northeast of the capital. Here, at Jericho, we see even more pilgrims joining Jesus and his group. Now, the crowds really swell. It becomes a triumphal procession as they move through the great city down the main street. It is like a grand parade with Christ leading the way.

But then, something happened. It was such a trifling incident, but no one ever forgot it. A blind man lived in Jericho; Bartimaeus was his name. He was a beggar who sat on the main street every day asking for money. Somehow or another, this blind man heard that Jesus of Nazareth was coming through his city and was about to pass by. Evidently, Bartimaeus knew who Jesus was and why everyone was so excited by his arrival. He had probably heard about the many great miracles Christ had performed.

Therefore, Bartimaeus now begins to shout at the top of his lungs, "Jesus, Son of David, have mercy on me! Jesus, Lord Messiah, help me!" Repeatedly he shouts this out. And Bartimaeus must have had a loud voice because those in the crowd near him finally said, "Hey, you old bum, shut up! Be quiet! You're spoiling the whole parade."

Mark says, "Many rebuked him and told him to be quiet, but he shouted even louder, 'Son of David, have mercy on me!'" Bartimaeus saw his chance and he was not about to quit. Jesus was coming and he knew that it was now or never.

When Christ came to the place where Bartimaeus was seated, he suddenly stopped. He stood still and the whole procession behind him stopped as well. The whole show came to a grinding halt. Silence fell so that the shouting of Bartimaeus became even more obvious. "Jesus, Son of David, have mercy on me!" was ringing through the crowded streets of Jericho.

"Call him," commanded Jesus. The people then told Bartimaeus, "Cheer up, old fellow! On your feet! He's calling you." Throwing his cloak aside, Bartimaeus jumped to his feet and was escorted over to where Jesus stood in the street.

And so, with the great crowds as spectators, these two men faced each other, the beggar with no light in his eyes and the man who was the Light of the World. Then, the question from Jesus' lips, "What do you want me to do for you?"

Bartimaeus simply says, "I want to see." You can almost feel the pain of being blind for so many years in those simple words. "I want to see. Lord, I want to be healed. I want to be made whole and restored. O Lord Jesus, help me!"

Christ sees the faith that Bartimaeus has. This is a faith that believes Jesus is the Messiah sent by God. He is the promised Son of David. He is the Lord who has compassion upon those who are suffering, and he has the power to heal and help and make all things new.

What follows now is interesting. No anointing occurs; there is no laying on of hands. But there are only the simple words of Christ which say, "Go, your faith has made you well." Immediately, Bartimaeus receives his eyesight back. The Lord speaks his Word and the blind man is healed. Just like that! Here, we see how God's Word is a Word of healing. It is a Word of salvation and restoration.

Literally, Christ says, "Go, your faith has saved you." Salvation brings healing and hope. Christ makes all things new. Faith believes this. Faith receives the gift of salvation and renewal to be found in Jesus the Messiah.

Mark tells us, "Immediately Bartimaeus received his sight and followed Jesus along the road." That's how it is. We receive the gift and then we respond in faith. We are healed and then immediately follow Christ along the road. That is what Bartimaeus did and that is what we do as well. We follow our Lord on the road to Jerusalem; we follow him into his suffering and death and into his resurrection.

Think about what probably happened to Bartimaeus after he was healed. We don't know for sure, but we can probably guess he joined the crowds going up to Jerusalem. He surely continued to follow this extraordinary man who had just healed him so miraculously. With seeing eyes, he joined the great procession as it left Jericho behind.

Imagine the joy and wonder of Bartimaeus as he looks for the first time upon the majestic city of David. Did it take his breath away to see the great city of God, to see the huge temple complex? Did he stay with the pilgrims who came up to celebrate the Passover at Jerusalem? Did he see Jesus ride in triumph on Palm Sunday? Did he witness how Christ cleared the temple of the moneychangers?

Did he hear about how Christ had been betrayed, arrested and taken away? Did he learn about how Jesus was put on trial and unfairly condemned as a criminal? Did he watch as Jesus was led out by the Romans to be crucified? Was he there at Golgotha on Good Friday? Was he there in the crowd, watching the slow and terrible death of Christ on the cross?

I think it's quite possible. Bartimaeus may have seen Jesus on the cross. He may have seen with his own eyes how the Lord suffered and died. He may have witnessed how Christ shed his holy and precious blood. Many people did that day.

Imagine what that must have been like for Bartimaeus to witness all these things. Imagine watching the Lord who had just opened your eyes being put to death by crucifixion. Imagine seeing the Son of God dying on a cross.

And yet, that is exactly what we have to see. We need to look with the eyes of faith and see our Savior on that cross. The truth is we will never truly understand why the Son of God came into this world until we see him on that cross outside of Jerusalem.

God has to open your eyes so that you can look with the eyes of faith and see your Lord on that cross. Then, you discover how he takes all your sins upon himself and he carries them all down into his terrible suffering and death.

Christ takes all of our guilt and sin down into his eternal death and there they die forever. They are put to death and are now gone forever. In Christ, you are forgiven! You are healed and restored. "By his wounds, we are healed." Christ makes all things new (and that includes you!)

When we see that, then we can say along with the Apostle Paul, "I have been crucified with Christ and I no longer live, but Christ lives in me. The life I live now, I live by faith in the Son of God, who loved me and gave himself for me. I now live for God."

That is what Bartimaeus could say. He could say, "I know my Savior loves me. He not only opened my eyes, but also he loved me and gave himself on the cross for me. And he has given me my sight back so that I could follow him. I now see with the eyes of faith that he truly is the Son of God. He is my Messiah!"

Look now with the eyes of faith and you will behold Jesus. Look and see how he is full of mercy and compassion. He cares about you and he wants to heal you and restore your sight so that you can look into the face of your Savior.

Do you see it? You can cry out to him in your suffering and distress. You can shout, "Jesus, Son of David, have mercy upon me! Lord, help me in my time of need!" And he will answer, "Cheer up! On your feet! What do you want for me to do for you?"

Then you answer, "Lord, I want to see! I want to witness the power of your cross at work in my life. I want to experience your love and grace and be made new. O Lord, I want to see!"

And Christ says, "Go! Your faith has saved you. You are healed and made new. Come now and follow me! Know that I am always with you; I will never leave you or forsake you. Together, we shall journey along the way until you enter the majestic city of God, the New Jerusalem that awaits all who trust in God's mercy." Amen!

HEAVENLY FOOD: John 6:41-69

In America, we have been richly blessed with plenty of food. Our country has an abundant food supply. Hunger and thirst are not really a problem for most people.

It has been said that by his 70th birthday, the average American consumes 15 cows, 25 hogs, 4 lambs and 1,000 chickens. Each year, the average American eats about 100 pounds of bread. We drink about 60 gallons of water a year and consume 45 gallons of soda and 20 gallons of beer. Now, that's a lot of food and drink!

At the beginning of the human race, Adam and Eve ate the forbidden fruit and that led to a perfect creation being spoiled and ruined. In Revelation, the Risen Christ says, "To him who overcomes, I will give the right to eat from the tree of life which is in the paradise of God." We see eating and drinking in the Bible from the beginning to the end, from Genesis to Revelation.

It is remarkable how often "food" is mentioned in the Bible. For example, the word "bread" is mentioned about 500 times. The first mention is when Melchizedek brings bread and wine to Abraham. Sarah serves bread to the three strangers that come to visit. Esau sells his birthright to Jacob for a dish of lentils and some bread. The Passover meal was eaten with unleavened bread. God fed the Israelites in the wilderness with manna from heaven. In the temple, the priests set out the 12 loaves of bread each week to symbolize God's presence with his people.

When we turn to the New Testament, we also see how bread is repeatedly mentioned. When Jesus was hungry in the wilderness, Satan tempts him to turn stones into bread. In the Lord's Prayer, we ask that God would give us "our daily bread." Jesus provides bread for over 5,000 people and then again for over 4,000.

And today, Jesus says, "I am the living bread that came down from heaven. If anyone eats of this bread, he will live forever. My flesh is true food and my blood is true drink. Whoever feeds on my flesh and drinks my blood has eternal life and I will raise him up on the last day."

Normally, we eat because we are hungry. We have an appetite and a craving for something good. And it's easy to work up an appetite, isn't it?

That's like when you go to Denny's and you look at those big fantastic menus with all the glossy color pictures of the food they serve. It makes you hungry just looking at the menu. Your mouth waters. Your stomach growls. You cannot wait to order. It all looks so good.

But what about our spiritual life? Are we spiritually hungry? Do we have a real appetite for the bread of life? Do we crave Jesus?

Sadly, I would say most people do not crave the bread of life. They have no spiritual life to speak of. They are kind of dead inside. They never think about God or the Bible or their soul. They are so wrapped up in their earthly life; they can never lift up their eyes to see something beyond the here and now. They never think about heaven.

But there are some people who hunger for something more than what this earthly life can offer. Way deep down inside, there is a hunger that says, "There must be something more to all this. There must be something better than just what I see around me. There's got to be a better life somewhere."

Some people are spiritually hungry. And you know what's that like. You have felt the hunger pangs. You have felt that emptiness inside. You have felt the sadness and grief of life in this fallen world. You have felt the guilt and regret that sin brings into our broken existence. You have felt the frustration of an unfair world, a world filled with injustice, falsehood and petty selfishness.

We have all felt that loneliness, unhappiness and restlessness way deep down inside. The truth is we are starving to death. We need food. We need nourishment.

Today, our Lord comes to us and he says, "I am the living bread that came down from heaven. If anyone eats of this bread, he will live forever. For my flesh is true food and my blood is true drink."

In other words, our Lord says, "I know you are spiritually hungry. I know you are looking for something true and lasting. Come now and feed upon me and I will satisfy your deepest need."

Jesus says, "Behold, I give myself for you! I suffer and die on the cross for you. I take away all of your sins forever. But come and partake of the bread of life. Receive my gift! The one who feeds on me will live because of me."

That's why it all comes down to Jesus Christ, the Son of God. He is the source of all true life. He is the center of our existence. He is the Alpha and Omega, the First and the Last, the Beginning and the End. If you have Jesus, you have life. If you believe in him, your sins are forgiven. If you put your faith in him, he will raise you up on the last day.

Notice how Christ specifically says, "Unless you eat the flesh of the Son of Man and drink his blood, you have no life in you." Our Lord points to himself as the Way. He is the source of all true life. It's all about Jesus.

That is why Holy Communion is so powerful and essential for our spiritual life. Some people ask, "What's the big deal about Holy Communion? Why should I go? What's the benefit of this eating and drinking? How can a little bit of bread and wine do anything for me? How is this going to help me?"

The benefit can be found in that Word which the Lord speaks to us at each and every celebration of Holy Communion. Jesus says, "This is my body given for you. This is my blood shed for the forgiveness of sins." The Lord speaks his Word and he bestows his gift. He feeds us with his body and blood. The Son of God feeds our hungry soul with the bread of life. He gives us true food and true drink. This is the bread that came down from heaven. Whoever feeds upon this heavenly food will live forever.

You see, the Lord's Supper is heavenly food for our soul. We eat and drink so that our faith might be nourished and strengthened. We receive the true body and blood of Christ and his gift is bestowed.

This is the gift we all desperately need. We all need to have our faith strengthened and nourished. The truth is we all struggle in our spiritual life. We often feel faint, weary and exhausted. We stumble in our spiritual life and fall. We have such a hard time believing and living out our faith.

For such times when our soul is hard pressed, the Lord's Supper brings true comfort and strength. It brings us sweet relief. Our Lord says, "Come and receive my body and blood. For my flesh is real food and my blood is real drink. Remain in me and I will remain in you."

Today, the Risen Lord invites you to come and receive his gift. He wants to give you that reassurance you are looking for. He wants to feed your hungry soul. He wants to bestow his comfort and peace. He wants to richly bless you today.

The bottom line is this: We can face life in this fallen world because we know that we have a better life awaiting us. We have the true and lasting life that only God can give. We have the promise that Christ will raise us up on the last day. We know that one day we will celebrate with all the saints the marriage feast of the Lamb in his kingdom that will never end. Heaven awaits!

Knowing that we are safe in God's presence, we now have strength and hope. We have that assurance of salvation we all need. We have Jesus, the Living Bread that came down from heaven. This is our loving Savior who says, "Whoever feeds upon me will live forever. My flesh is true food and my blood is true drink. Come and partake of the bread of life!" Amen!

THE NARROW ROAD: Mark 8:27-38

Imagine how Peter must have felt. Try to put yourself in his position. If you were Peter, you would say:

I felt great. I had just told Jesus that he was the Christ, the promised Messiah. We had been traveling up north in the region of Caesarea Philippi. Jesus had asked us, "Who do the people say that I am?"

We gave the usual answers. Some people thought Jesus was a great prophet, or perhaps even John the Baptist come back from the dead. That's when Jesus looked directly into my eyes. He said, "But what about you, Peter? Who do you think I am?"

That's when I answered, "You are the Christ." I must admit I felt good about my answer. But then I was surprised and shocked when Jesus said, "Things are going to change now." Jesus deeply sighed. He looked sad.

We all were walking with him toward a small spring of water. He then said, "I have to go to Jerusalem. When I get there, I will be rejected by the people. I will suffer many things from the elders and the chief priests and the scribes. I'm telling you now so that you won't be surprised when it happens. But it will happen."

Jesus knelt down by the spring of water bubbling up from the ground. He made a cup of his hands and scooped the water. Just before he started to drink, he turned to us and said, "I will be killed in Jerusalem, and on the third day be raised."

That's when I reacted. I grabbed his wrist and shouted, "No!" The water splashed from his hands. "No," I cried, "God won't allow it! This can never happen to you!"

But then Jesus said to me, "Get behind me, Satan! For you are not setting your mind on the things of God, but on the things of man."

I cried out, "No, Lord, I do care about the things of God! But this is all so confusing for me. One minute I'm Peter; the next minute I'm Satan. I'm so confused! I don't understand what's happening."

Poor Peter! Can you identify with his frustration? Can you understand why he is confused? You see, Peter loved the Lord Jesus, but he could not understand the narrow road Christ was talking about.

Jesus came to go the narrow way of the cross. The road that Peter wanted to travel was the way of the world. It was the broad road to glory, success, power, fame and riches. Peter thought the Messiah was supposed to be a powerful, worldly figure, not someone who would suffer and be rejected.

Here, we are often like Peter. We may love the Lord, but we lose our way. It's hard for us to follow the way of Christ. The narrow road is difficult. We stumble and fall. One minute, we are a child of God; the next minute, we are a child of the devil. We have such drastic ups and downs in our spiritual life. Sometimes, we feel like such utter failures. We don't know what to do.

That is precisely why the Lord directs us to the narrow road. The broad road the world rushes down is ultimately a dead end. If we put our hope in worldly glory, success and power, then we will surely be disappointed. Such things are temporary at best. They will always fail us in the end. What good is it if we gain the whole world but forfeit our soul?

In the Sermon on the Mount, Jesus says, "Enter through the narrow gate. For wide is the gate and broad is the road that leads to destruction, and many enter through it. But small is the gate and narrow the road that leads to life, and only a few find it."

Today, Jesus confronts us with the message of the narrow road. He says, "If anyone would come after me, let him deny himself and take up his cross and follow me. For whoever would save his life will lose it, and whoever loses his life for my sake will save it."

Jesus says, "Follow me on this narrow way. Leave behind the well-worn path of the world, and follow the path of God." Christ says, "I want you to surrender your life. Give it all to me! I don't want only half of it, but everything. I want you and all of you! No half-measures are good enough here."

The Lord says, "Hand over your whole self, warts and all. Give me the whole package. Don't forget to include all your sins, guilt and regrets. Give me everything that's bad and messed-up in your life. Give it all to me, and I will give you back a new self and a new life."

And so, the Lord Jesus takes our old life and he carries it down that narrow road. He takes us to the cross. We lose our old life in his suffering and death, and we then discover something new.

However, it all begins with the narrow path that the Son of God must travel. The Christ must suffer many things. He must be rejected and be killed. Jesus will go to Jerusalem and suffer the passion. Christ goes to the Garden of Gethsemane on that dark evening before Good Friday. There, in that garden, Jesus is betrayed by Judas. He is arrested and taken away. They lead him through the narrow streets of Jerusalem.

Our Lord is then examined by the high priests, Annas and Caiaphas. He is afterwards taken away to Pontius Pilate. At his trial, Jesus is falsely accused of many crimes. Even though he is innocent and had done nothing wrong, Pilate condemns Jesus to suffer death by execution. First, he is scourged and flogged. Then, the soldiers mock him with a purple robe and a crown of thorns. They slap him and spit in his face. Finally, they take Jesus away.

The Roman soldiers force him to carry his cross through the narrow streets. The battered and bleeding Messiah collapses on the way. Someone from the crowd is forced to bear the cross and follow Jesus as he makes his way to Golgotha. There, they crucify him, nailing him to the wood.

As he hangs on the cross, the Christ is mocked by the elders and the chief priests and the scribes. They pour their scorn and ridicule upon him. Finally, Jesus breathes his last. He dies. Darkness covers the land. Quickly, the body of Christ is taken down from the cross and placed in a tomb. The narrow road has ended in death and burial.

Nevertheless, we know that this is not the end of the road for Jesus the Messiah. The tomb is but the narrow gate that leads to eternal life. It is but a gateway to the resurrection. It is the road to the brand new life that our Lord gives.

This is the narrow road of Jesus the Messiah. He takes us down the pathway of his passion; he leads us to his cross and suffering and death. Then, we go with Christ to the tomb and burial. After three days, we emerge into the bright sunlight of Easter morning. This is the narrow road we travel by faith.

Paul says, "I have been crucified with Christ and I no longer live, but Christ lives in me. The life I live now, I live by faith in the Son of God, who loved me and gave himself for me."

That's how it is! You were crucified with Christ. Your sins died with him on the cross. The life you have right now, you have by faith in the Son of God. He is the one who loved you so much that he gave himself on the cross for you.

And today, Jesus says, "Come and follow me. Come and give yourself to me. Don't hold back! Give yourself totally to me. I will now enable you to travel down the narrow road. I will walk with you and teach you to set your mind on the things of God. I will show you how to live by faith."

But still, we say, "Lord, I do love you and I do want to follow. However, sometimes I'm like Peter. I have such a hard time understanding why things happen the way they do. I lose my faith so easily. I'm up and then I'm down. Sometimes, I feel like such an utter failure."

That's when Jesus looks us right in the eye, and he says, "I know. That's why I went to the cross for you. But that's also why I rose from the dead – to give you a new life where your sins are forgiven each day, and where the light of Easter morning shines continually upon you every day."

The Lord says, "Come on, let's go walk together down this narrow road. Come on, I will help you along the way. With my help, you can make it. Together, we will travel the road that leads all the way to eternal salvation." Amen!

GETTING DOWN TO BUSINESS:
Luke 19:28-40

A ten-year-old schoolboy wasn't doing so well in math. His parents decided to enroll their son in a private Catholic school. The boy stormed home the first day of school, went straight up to his room and closed the door. Two hours later, he emerged for a quick meal, announced he was studying again and went straight back to his room to study until bedtime.

He did this every day, right through the first term. Then, one day after school, the boy came home with his report card, dropped it on the family dinner table, and went straight up to his room. His parents cautiously opened the report card and couldn't believe their eyes. They saw an "A" besides the line that read "Mathematics." Excitedly, they ran up to their son's room.

The father asked, "Was it the nuns?" The boy shook his head and said, "No." "Was it the special tutoring?" asked the mother. Again, the boy shook his head. "Was it the special textbooks?" "No." "Well, what was it?" the parents asked.

The boy then said, "From the first day of school, I knew these folks were serious about math. When I walked into the entrance of the main building and I saw a guy nailed to a big plus sign, I knew they really meant business!"

Today, we get down to business. Or rather, we see how the Son of God gets down to business. On the cross, the Son of God got serious about our sin and salvation. He meant business when he came to earth as a baby born in a stable in Bethlehem. Christ really rolled up his sleeves and got down to work.

The Son of God meant business when he healed the sick, raised the dead, calmed troubled souls, comforted the grieving and reached out to those whom no one else cared about. He was serious about bringing God's salvation to a lost world. He got to work in rescuing a world that is perishing. And finally, in the very end, the Son of God was nailed to a cross for the sin of the whole world. He died for all the sin and guilt and failure of every single person who ever lived.

Today, we hear how Jesus rode into Jerusalem on Palm Sunday. This reading from Luke kicks off our season of Advent in a big way. Right after Jesus did this, he told the people, "The hour has come for the Son of Man to be glorified. Now is the time for judgment on this world, now the prince of this world will be driven out. But I, when I am lifted up from the earth, will draw all men to myself."

Our Lord speaks of being lifted up on a cross. The question is sometimes asked, "Why do you Christians make such a big deal about the cross?" Indeed, what's so special about this death that happened over 2,000 years ago, in a place so far away? What's the big deal about a dead Jew on a cross?

The answer is this: God takes sin and salvation seriously. The Bible tells us that sin is serious. It is a deadly problem for all of us. All of us, from the tiniest newborn baby to oldest senior citizen, have this innate desire to do what is wrong. We are born into this world as sinners. We find it much easier to do what is wrong than to do what is right and true. Sin comes to us naturally, so to speak. "Flesh gives birth to flesh."

To put it another way, we can say, "No one is perfect." That is, no one is the way God intends humans to be. We sometimes say no one is perfect as an excuse for the all the mistakes we make. However, when the Bible says no one is perfect, that's not an excuse but a statement of reality. Jesus says, "Be perfect as your heavenly Father is perfect." Peter says, "Be holy as God is holy." Paul says, "All have sinned and fall short of the glory of God."

Some of us may try to ignore all this. We may pretend there is nothing wrong. However, the hard reality of sin shows itself in the things we think and desire. It reveals itself in what we say and do. We do stupid and foolish things. We say such hurtful words. We fail to be the kind of people God wants us to be.

That's why we are often filled with regret and remorse. We struggle with a guilty conscience. When we see the hurt we inflict on others, we realize that sin does have serious consequences. And the greatest consequence is that sin destroys our relationship with God. It separates us from the source of all true life and hope.

Remember, God created humans to be perfect and to live in peace and harmony. We were originally created to have a perfect relationship with other people and with our Creator. Our rebellion ruined all that. The fall of Adam and Eve destroyed what we had in the beginning. Sin brought death and misery, pain and woe. "The wages of sin is death."

However, let's be clear. God takes no pleasure in that fact that sin has taken control of our lives. God is not pleased that we have all fallen away from him. God takes no pleasure in sin and death. That is exactly why God gets down to business to do something about our sorry state. God sends his Son to rescue and deliver us.

You see, God the Father loves you so very much that he sent his Son to die for you on a cross, to die in your place and to suffer your judgment. On the cross, the Son of God takes upon himself all of our sin and guilt.

Paul says it so simply, "He died for all." Jesus died for all people. On the cross, he died for every person who has ever lived in the past, those who are living today and all who will live in the future. No one is excluded. He died for all. His love reaches out to all. "But I, when I am lifted up from the earth, will draw all men to myself." And there is no greater truth than that. "He died for all."

Now we reach the point where we get down to some serious business. You can know all about the historical facts about the cross and resurrection of Jesus, but that's not enough. You can know all about the birth of Jesus in Bethlehem, but that's not enough. You can know that Jesus suffered under Pontus Pilate, was crucified, died and was buried - but still, something can still be missing. There is one more step to take.

You still need to get down to business and you have to make the cross and resurrection your very own. In other words, you need to come to the point of personal faith. You need to make a real commitment to Christ.

You need to confess, "He died and rose again FOR ME! He died to free me from sin, death and hell. Christ is my personal Savior!" This is where you boldly confess before the whole world, "I believe in Jesus Christ, the Son of God. I trust in him. I know I belong to him forevermore."

This need for a total commitment to Christ is illustrated in the following story. It was Sunday morning in South America. In a little church on the border of Venezuela and Colombia, a worship service was beginning. Suddenly, a band of Communist guerrillas armed with machine guns came bursting out of the jungle. They crashed and banged their way into the little church. The pastor and congregation were stunned. The guerrillas dragged the pastor outside to be executed.

Then, the leader of the rebels came back into the chapel and demanded, "Anyone else who believes in all this Christian nonsense, come forward!" Everyone was petrified. They were frozen. There was a long silence.

Finally, one man came forward and stood in front of the rebel leader. He simply said, "I believe in Jesus." The man was then roughly tossed to the soldiers and taken out to be executed. Several other people then came forward and said the same thing. They were also driven outside.

Suddenly, there was the sound of machine gun fire. When there were no more people inside the church willing to identify themselves as Christians, the guerrilla chief told the remaining congregation to get out. "Get out!" he said. "You have no right to be here!" With that, he herded them out of the building.

When the people got outside, they were astonished to see their pastor and the others standing there. The pastor and those people were ordered to go back inside the church to continue the worship service while the others were warned to stay out. The guerrilla leader then said, "You stay out here until you have the courage to stand up for your beliefs." And with that, the rebels disappeared into the jungle.

So too, we can ask the question, "Do we have the right to be here today? Do we have the courage to stand up for our beliefs?" I mean, do you believe in Christ as your Savior? Do you really believe? Are you willing to stake your life on it? Are you totally committed to the Savior who lived and died for you? Do you trust that his death on the cross truly takes away all of your sins? Do you believe his resurrection gives you a new life, a life that will last forever?

If so, then you are ready to get down to business and live out your faith each day. You can now live in faith, hope and trust. You can experience that new life that Christ gives you. You can rejoice and be glad in God's salvation.

Now, we are able by God's grace to follow Jesus and joyfully confess our faith to the entire world. We now share the good news that Christ died for all. We seek to love others as God has loved us. We roll up our sleeves and get to work. We reach to others and share the gift we have received.

Like the crowds on Palm Sunday who welcomed Jesus into Jerusalem, we welcome our King. He comes to us in mercy and grace. He comes to rescue lost sinners. He comes to restore to us everlasting life. He comes to take care of business.

The King of all creation has arrived and things will never be the same. Christ comes to go the cross for us and to make all things new. He comes to bring us courage and hope. In Christ, we are able to stand firm in the faith. We can endure and be strong in the Lord.

Therefore, let us rejoice and celebrate. "Blessed is the King who comes to us in the name of the Lord! Hosanna in the highest! Blessed is Christ, our personal Savior!" Amen!

A CHRISTMAS LETTER FROM MARY: Luke 1:26-38

At this time of the year, we once again hear the story of Mary. We join her today in praising God for the wondrous gift of the Christ Child. Mary plays a very special part in the Christmas story. Today, we share with you "A Christmas Letter from Mary." The letter begins:

My dear friends,

Let me tell you about the events that took place that first Christmas. I lived with my parents in a little town called Nazareth in Galilee. Back then, girls were often engaged in their early teens. I was engaged to Joseph, the local carpenter. I was young but very happy. Joseph was the kindest man in Nazareth. We were looking forward to our wedding day.

Then, one day out of the blue, an angel appeared to me. He glowed so brightly, I could hardly look at him. I was so afraid. I had never seen an angel before. He introduced himself as Gabriel, and said, "Greetings, you who are highly favored! The Lord is with you! I have a special message for you from God." When Gabriel told me what that message was I nearly fainted.

He said, "Do not be afraid, Mary; you have found favor with God. You will be with child and will give birth to a son, and you are to give him the name, Jesus."

Now, try to understand my situation. My cousin Elizabeth was going to have a baby, even though she were very old and never had children before. However, she was married to Zachariah the priest and had been so for a long time. And here I was - single – and engaged to be married to Joseph. How could such a pregnancy be a sign of God's favor?

Nevertheless, the angel went on, "Your son will be great and will be called the Son of the Most High. The Lord God will give him the throne of his father David, and he will reign over the house of Jacob forever. His kingdom will never end. Your baby will be the promised Messiah, the Son of David, the true King of Israel!"

I don't know whether I caught that last part because I was still in shock when I heard, "You will become pregnant and will give birth to a son." Our society was not very kind to unmarried mothers. Moreover, what would Joseph say? And how would my parents react? What about my friends? What would people say when they found out?

Nevertheless, while I had all my questions, I sensed that God was planning something very special. And God was going to do it through me! Therefore, I responded to Gabriel by saying, "I am the Lord's servant; may it be to me as you have said."

I really didn't understand everything that was about to happen to me, but I was ready to obey the Lord's will. If this was God's promise to me, I was willing to have faith and to trust that God knew what was best for me.

I was so excited for a while, but then, reality hit me. How was I going to tell Joseph that I was pregnant? What was I going to say to him? As the days went by, I tried to work out what I would say. But no matter what words I used, they all sounded wrong.

I tried to pick the right moment. So one evening, as we watched the sunset, I told Joseph about the angel Gabriel and his message. I then told Joseph that I was pregnant and would have a baby boy. I just couldn't hide the excitement in my voice.

Poor Joseph went silent. I could see that he was struggling to take everything in that I had just said to him. He was such a kind, sweet man. Furthermore, Joseph was very well known in our area. People would assume the worst. They would talk. His family would be upset and ashamed. His business might even be ruined.

Therefore, it didn't really surprise me when he said he couldn't believe my story. He was breaking off our engagement. He just could not marry me. I could feel the hurt in his voice, but he wasn't mean about it. Clearly, he felt bad and upset about the whole situation. It was a real mess.

However, the next day, he came to my house all excited. When he had calmed down, he told me what had just happened. He said he tried to go back to work, but couldn't concentrate. All that night, he tossed and turned. He finally fell into a deep sleep and had a strange dream.

In that dream, an angel appeared to him, and said, "Joseph, the baby that Mary will have is from the Holy Spirit. Go ahead and marry her! Then, after her baby is born, give him the name Jesus because he will save his people from their sins."

Joseph now totally believed my story about Gabriel. And so, it was true! This baby growing within me was a special gift from God. This child is the Son of God, and he will be called Jesus because he will save all people from their sins.

Joseph might not have been the actual father of Jesus, but I can tell you that he was as excited as any father could be. And I was excited, too. All that Joseph told me confirmed that this really was from God. However, what happened next, made life very difficult for us.

That Roman emperor, Caesar Augustus, ordered that a census be taken. He wanted to tax everyone, so everyone had to return to their place of birth to be counted. Since we were both from Bethlehem, this would mean a long trip from Nazareth to go down there. Bethlehem is just a little south of Jerusalem.

Remember, we didn't have cars or trains back then. We traveled everywhere on foot. In addition, by this time, I was heavily pregnant. I can tell you, I thought we would never get there. However, at the same time, I knew that God would not let anything happen to the precious child I was carrying.

When we finally got to Bethlehem, it was so crowded. There was no place to stay anywhere. Finally, we found shelter in a stable where they kept the animals for the night. No sooner had Joseph put down some fresh straw, I went into labor. Joseph did a marvelous job in delivering a beautiful baby boy. He then found a manger that made a very nice crib.

Not too long after this, I looked up and saw Joseph leading in a group of untidy, rough-looking characters. They turned out to be a bunch of shepherds from the nearby fields, and they had a marvelous story about angels who had appeared to them.

The angels had announced that a Savior has been born - he is Christ the Lord. They then knelt beside the manger and quietly looked at my baby. As they left, they thanked us and said that this was a night they would never forget.

There is a lot more I could tell you. I am just so glad that God chose me to be the mother of Jesus, and Joseph to be his earthly father. Who would ever have thought that God would use two ordinary people like us to raise a boy who would bring salvation to the whole world?

We knew that this boy was very special. However, we would have never guessed what would happen in the end. We all were surprised when, as a young man, Jesus quit his job as a carpenter and started to travel about the countryside, preaching about the kingdom of God. He started working incredible miracles and healing the sick. Large crowds began to follow him. Frankly, I didn't know what to think.

On the one hand, I was so excited that my son was now doing the work of the Messiah; on the other hand, I was so very afraid. Many powerful and influential people didn't like Jesus or the message he was preaching. In fact, rumors began to circulate that some people wanted to stop him at any cost. But my son was not afraid. He was determined to keep on going. He told me, "I must do my Father's will." (And I knew he wasn't talking about Joseph).

I must admit, I did not fully understand everything Jesus was talking about. However, I was there at the very end. I was there when he died.

I followed him to Jerusalem for that last, fateful Passover. I watched everything that happened after Jesus was betrayed by Judas and arrested in the Garden of Gethsemane. I watched as they put him on trial, and as he was flogged and scourged by the Romans. I followed him through the streets of Jerusalem as he carried the cross out to the place where they crucified him. I watched as they pounded the iron spikes through his hands and feet.

I saw the suffering and pain that was inflicted on my son. It stung me deeply. I stood there at the foot of the cross for all those long hours. No parent likes to see their child suffer. But I knew that the boy that God placed in my life was sent for a very special purpose.

I now know that it was necessary for the Messiah to suffer in this way. Jesus had to die on that cross to be our Savior. He had to suffer to save us from our sins. He had to die so that we might live. He had to suffer to give us the hope of life everlasting. The Messiah gave himself for us, to pay the price for our sins.

Some have asked me, if I would have known what would happen to Jesus at the end, would I still have been so willing to give birth to this child and to raise him. That is a hypothetical question, but I like to think that yes, I would have said, "I am the Lord's servant, may it be to me as you have said."

I am so glad that God gave me the faith to trust his plan for my life. And I'll tell you, it took lots of faith to be the Lord's servant. Obeying God's Word was not easy for me. And I know the same is true for you.

We don't know what the future hold for us. We don't know what's going to happen next year or in the years ahead. There will be times of sickness and health, times of success and failure, times of great happiness and deep sorrow.

We may not understand why some things turn out the way they do. Things happen that break our heart. Things happen that test our faith and loyalty to God. So many things can cause our hearts to be filled with fear and worry.

However, we need to simply trust that God is in control. God knows what he is doing and he promises to love us, watch over us, forgive us, and in the end, take us to himself in heaven.

What we need to do is simply say, "Yes, I am the Lord's servant! I believe your promises, God. May it be to me as you have said." We need to have faith and commit our whole life to God's care.

Always remember how God the Father sent his Son into this world. Christ is the true Messiah and the Savior of all. As the angel told Joseph, he is "Immanuel" which means, "God is with us."

As you celebrate Jesus' birthday again this year, remember that Christ is with you. Remember why the Son of God came into this world as a baby. Remember how Jesus loves you! He suffered and died for you. He shed his holy and precious blood to take away all of your sins. Then, he rose from the dead to give you the best Christmas gift ever – eternal life in God's new creation. And may God richly bless you all this Christmastime! Amen!

Love, Mary.

*Here is a bonus sermon from the book
The Key is Love*

A SHORT SERMON: Mark 5:21-43

Today, we have a short sermon. No long, boring message. I'm just going to keep it short and simple today. There will be no stories or dumb jokes.

I'm not going to tell the story of how one day the big fence between heaven and hell broke down. St. Peter appeared at the broken section of the fence to inspect it. When he saw the devil walking over, he shouted, "Hey, Satan! How about getting your crew to fix this broken fence?"

The devil says, "We're busy over here. We can't fix your lousy fence." Peter answered, "If you don't, I'm going to file a lawsuit against you." The devil laughed, and said, "Oh yeah? And where are you going to find a lawyer?"

I'm also not going to mention how three guys on motorcycles pulled into a truck stop. Inside, there was only one customer, a truck driver quietly eating his dinner. He was a little guy, kind of meek looking.

The three bikers come over and start harassing him. One guy knocks his cap off, the other guy puts his cigarette out in his coffee, and the third one grabbed his plate of food and took it away.

The truck driver said nothing. He got up, paid for his dinner and left. One of the bikers, disappointed that they couldn't provoke a reaction from the little guy, commented to the waitress, "He wasn't much of a man, was he?"

The waitress replied, "No, I guess not." Then, looking out the window, she added, "I guess he's not much of a truck driver either. He just ran over three motorcycles."

Today, we skip such stories and jokes and go right to our reading. As we do so, we see how Jesus is surrounded by a great crowd that was following him. Our Lord was a source of hope to so many people, people who were desperate and in need of help.

One such person was Jairus, the father of a girl who was sick and dying. Jairus came to Jesus and said, "My little daughter is at the point of death. Can you come and lay your hands on her so that she may be made well and live?"

Christ immediately responds. He says, "Let's go!" And so, they start to work their way through the crowd. You know what that's like, trying to move through a big crowd of people all packed tightly together.

Now there was a woman in this crowd. She had a serious health problem, some kind of internal bleeding that wouldn't clear up. She was desperate, too.

She had heard about Jesus and how he had the power to help and heal the sick. And so she decides she's going to try to meet Jesus or at least try to reach out and touch him as he goes by. She said to herself, "If I touch even his garments, I will be made well."

Now, that's faith! Faith says, "Jesus has the power to help and heal. I'm going to reach out to him and trust he can help me in my situation."

This woman actually was able to touch the garments of Christ as he passed by and immediately she was healed. Jesus realized what had happened. He stops and addresses the people around him.

"Who touched me?" Jesus asks the crowd. The healed woman finally steps forward and confesses to Christ what she had done. And the Lord smiled and said, "Daughter, your faith has made you well! Go in peace and be healed of your disease."

But while Jesus was still speaking, some bad news came from the house of Jairus. His daughter had died. It was all over. She's dead. Gone forever.

Some people there even say, "Well, why bother the teacher anymore? Why bother? Jesus can't do anything now."

These people lack faith. They don't get it. You see, Jesus is more than just a teacher or great prophet. He is the very Son of God. He has the power to help and heal. He also has the power to give life to the dead.

But these people do not believe. They do not have faith. So they are willing to give up and quit. "Why bother any more? What can he do, anyway?"

But Christ says to Jairus, "Do not be afraid. All is not lost. Only believe! Have faith that I can help you." Then, the Lord says, "Let's go!"

When they get to the house of Jairus they confront a crowd of mourners carrying on. Jesus says, "Why are you making such a commotion? The child is not dead, but only sleeping." And the people laugh at him.

The Lord tells them, "All is not lost. I can still help." But the people laugh at Jesus. Again, we see the reaction of unbelief. People who lack faith laugh at the claims of Christ.

But Jesus immediately goes to where the dead girl is. He goes over to her, takes her hand and says, "Little girl, I say to you, arise!" And the girl sits up, alive! She then got up and walked around. Everyone is amazed. Jesus reaches out to this dead girl with his healing touch and she is made alive again.

But that's how it is: Christ is the healer and the giver of life. He is the Son of God who has the power to help and save, to deliver and rescue.

This is the compassionate Savior who cares about people who are hurting. He has great compassion for people who are facing a desperate situation. Jesus reaches out to people who are in great need, people like the woman who was bleeding and Jairus.

Listen, the Lord loves you and cares for you. He reaches out to you today in love and compassion. In fact, Christ loves you so much he was willing to lay aside his divine power and glory.

The Son of God humbled himself and made himself to be nothing. He was willing to go the cross to pay the price for our sins. He bled (just like the woman who was bleeding) and he died (just like the daughter of Jairus). Here we see how the Son of God shared our mortal life. He bled; he died; he suffers for us.

But through his passion, we receive healing and help. We receive forgiveness, life and salvation. And when we reach out to Christ in faith, we discover that he has already reached out to us first. Jesus reaches out to us in mercy and he says, "I say to you, get up, arise! Receive my gift of life."

Faith knows that Christ has the power to heal, to save and to give life. And so, we continue to reach out to him, no matter what our circumstances may be. We don't give up. We don't quit.

We continue to live by faith each day because we know Jesus loves us and he cares. Christ has mercy and compassion for all people, including you and me and everyone else.

And today, the Lord says, "Do not be afraid! Only believe. Trust that I love you and I care for you. Go now, your faith has made you well. Go in peace and continue to live by faith each day!" Amen!

Then Jesus called the crowd to himself along with his disciples and said, "If anyone would come after me, he must deny himself and take up his cross and follow me. For whoever wants to save his life will lose it, but whoever loses his life for me and for the gospel will save it."

"What good is it for a man to gain the whole world, yet forfeit his soul? Or what can a man give in exchange for his soul? If anyone is ashamed of me and my words in this adulterous and sinful generation, the Son of Man will be ashamed of him when he comes in his Father's glory with the holy angels."

Mark 8:34-38

And I heard a loud voice from the throne saying, "Now the dwelling of God is forever with his people. He will wipe every tear from their eyes. There will be no more death or mourning or crying or pain, for the old order of things has passed away."

God, who was seated on the throne, then said, "I am making everything new! Write this down, for all these words are trustworthy and true."

Revelation 21:3-5

Jesus said, "I am the true vine, and my Father is the gardener. He cuts off every branch in me that bears no fruit, while every branch that does bear fruit, he prunes so that it will be even more fruitful. Remain in me and I will remain in you. No branch can bear fruit by itself; it must remain in the vine. Neither can you bear fruit unless you remain in me."

"I am the vine; you are the branches. If anyone remains in me, they will bear much fruit; apart from me, you can do nothing. If anyone does not remain in me, he is like a branch that is thrown away."

"If you remain in me and my words remain in you, ask whatever you wish, and it will be given you. This is to my Father's glory, that you bear much fruit, showing yourselves to be my disciples."

John 15:1-8

Humble yourselves, therefore, under God's mighty hand, that he may lift you up in due time. Cast all your anxiety on him because he cares for you. Be self-controlled and alert. Your enemy the devil prowls around like a roaring lion looking for someone to devour. Resist him, standing firm in the faith.

1 Peter 5:6-9

ABOUT THE AUTHOR:

Volker Heide graduated from the United States Merchant Marine Academy in Kings Point, New York in 1982. (B.S., Nautical Science) and worked in the offshore oil industry. He graduated from Concordia Seminary in St. Louis, Missouri in 1990. (M.Div., New Testament Theology).

He has been a parish pastor in the Lutheran Church – Missouri Synod for almost 30 years, and has served churches in Mississippi and Connecticut. He is married to his wife, Ellen, and they have two daughters, Melissa and Kristen.

Made in the USA
Middletown, DE
19 May 2019